Sami Culture in a New Era

Acknowledgements
Davvi Girji o.s. would like to acknowledge the Sami Cultural Council, the
Norwegian Foreign Ministry, the Norwegian Research Council, and the
University of Tromsø for their financial support of this book. Likewise we
are also grateful for the support the editor has received from the
Norwegian Non-fiction Writers and Translators Association for this project.

Distributed in North America
by the University of Washington Press,
P.O. Box 50096, Seattle, WA 98145

© Copyright Davvi Girji, N-9730 Kárášjohka/Karasjok
Computer typeset by Davvi Girji OS, Kárášjohka/Karasjok, Norway
Cover photos: (top) Harry Johansen, Visot, Guovdageaidnu/Kautokeino.
Coverdesign: Davvi Girji OS.

Printed in Finland at Ykkös-Offset Oy, Vaasa.

ISBN 82-7374-354-3

Harald Gaski (ed.)

Sami Culture in a New Era

The Norwegian Sami Experience

Davvi Girji OS 1997

Editor's Preface

When I applied for a small grant from the Norwegian Non-fiction Writers and Translators Association many years ago to put together this collection of essays on contemporary Sami cultural issues in Norway, I did not know what a lengthy project I was about to involve myself in. The book has taken so much more time to finalize than I had ever expected – and still includes no more than ten essays. From my original letter of invitation to potential contributors until the final version of the book, the snow outside my windows has melted and returned many times. I know, not least through my own experience, that Sami scholars are extremely busy, occupied with practical and political assignments in addition to their academic obligations. I am therefore grateful to the contributing researchers and wish to thank them for their articles which make this collection of essays on contemporary Sami life in Norway quite broad in scope. I hope it provides a little piece of sought after information about the indigenous population of Northern Fennoscandia.

From my rather extensive traveling and lecturing different places in the world, I have on the one hand been astonished by the huge international interest there actually is for the Sami, and, on the other hand I have learnt that there is an enormous lack of information and teaching material designed for colleges and universities about my people and our culture. Therefore I took it as a challenge to contribute actively to improve the situation by offering to put together this book. At this stage – and also because of the strains and difficulties finding people who could find time to submit articles for this project – I decided quite early to limit the presentations to Sami issues in Norway, where the majority of the Sami people live. At a later stage, there ought to be developed a series of books introducing Sami culture and societal life at a wide range for an international audience.

Every essay in this book concentrates on one specific aspect of contemporary Sami society for a more detailed treatment. With the fairly wide division between different disciplines such as social-anthropology, history, linguistics, land management, education, literary criticism, mass media, and health care, the book is meant to offer a rather comprehensive introduction to a variety of Sami themes. The fact that most of the contributors are Sami themselves should further vouch for an active involvement and standing from the contributors' point of view with regards to the topics presented. An additional observation worth paying attention to is the up-to-date-ness of the articles; all of them deal with current issues which are being discussed among the Sami today, so what is offered here is a kind of a state-of-the-art report on contemporary Sami studies in Norway. We get acquainted with the background and the context for the internal Sami debate, but at the same time we see how these views are communicated to the outside world.

Today, no minority can survive in isolation; we need to make the rest of the world see us, and actively support the development of the indigenous peoples' culture, language and societal life – in the Arctic cold as well as in the depth of the jungle or the heat of the desert.

Table of Contents

Harald Gaski

Introduction:
Sami Culture in a New Era

In this introduction I will try to create a background for the following essays by saying something about Sami culture, identity and
sense of belonging, viewed from the inside by an active member of
a minority culture. I will try to do this by presenting some of the
conditions within Sami cultural life that have been and continue to
be important for the maintenance of Sami culture and identity. This
means that I will deal with circumstances that have made and still
make it possible for the Sami to practice their culture productively
and thereby develop, confirm, and demonstrate their identity, both
to themselves and to the outside world. I proceed in this manner,
not to reject or downplay the significance of Sami political objectives, but rather because of an awareness that these objectives primarily have been and still are founded on the desire to establish the
best possible conditions "for the Sami to develop their language,
their culture and their communal life," as stated in the amendment
to the Norwegian constitution, a document in which the Sami are
recognized as an indigenous people within Norway's borders.

Sami policy has never been directed toward the establishment
of a separate Sami nation state. Instead, it has concentrated more on
establishing rights that will assure the survival and growth of the
Sami and their culture in their own ancestral areas of settlement.
Even during periods of the most aggressive colonization and assimilation, as well as during the Christianization by force that took place
in the eighteenth and nineteenth centuries, the Sami turned to their
own cultural expressions as an internal defense against external
pressure. The Sami traditional form of musical expression, the *yoik*,

became a medium for inside agitation among the Sami, challenging them to resist the demands of the colonizers that they give up their language and culture. Even if they lost their right to the land, they would never give up their right to have intrinsic value and Sami-ness (Gaski 1993: 120-22). The *yoik* was chosen as a form of expression not only because of its central position among the Sami, but also because the yoik had a subtle system of double meanings and metaphorical imagery. It was necessary to camouflage the *yoik*'s political content because some of the public officials had acquired an elementary knowledge of the Sami language and could, therefore, suppress oppositional activities that were too obvious.

This also provides some historical background for the fact that the Sami focused so intently on the importance of language and artistic cultural expressions during the first stages of their political mobilization at the beginning of the twentieth century. The concepts of art and culture are relatively new to the Sami, but we can assume that what they encompass has been recognized so that art and culture have been manifested according to the Sami people's own understanding of their implications long before the terms became part of the language. In the rhetoric of cultural policy as well the theme has long been to preserve and develop Sami culture, a fact which would confirm that one at least has had a sense of what culture meant. "Culture" is a loan word into the Sami language. There is no traditional concept that covers the whole spectrum of meanings of activities which comprise the components of "culture". The closest one can come is *Sámi vuohki* which is best translated "Sami ways", that is, way of being, way of living, mentality and values. "Art" is called *dáidda* in Sami, in contrast to applied art and handcrafts, for which the term is *duodji. Dáidda* is in this context a new Sami word for that which is ordinarily defined as art, that is, "art" as opposed to "craft". Modern *duodji*-products are works of art in both form and craftsmanship, but, traditionally, *duodji* has always been connected with the object's practical function, which is not solely to be displayed for its esthetic qualities but rather to be used in everyday life. (Guttorm 1995: 153-56). It is a fact, however, that even among the Sami handcrafted items are more and more often becoming objects for display instead of for practical use.

There is, however, an important connection between *duodji* and *dáidda,* from applied art to art in the modern sense. *Duodji* comprises creative activities which are both intellectual and material, so a writer can equally well be called a *sátneduojár,* a Sami word meaning a crafter of words, or *girječálli,* a writer of books. Artists like Iver Jåks, Aage Gaup and Ingunn Utsi receive inspiration from the *duodji*-tradition for their sculptures. The principle behind their esthetic is to use organic materials, allowing wooden sculptures to be exposed to wind and weather and eventually decompose and disappear without a trace. In a way, this is parallel to the traditional Sami relationship with the natural environment, where the hand of nature erases all traces of Sami migration and settlement, perhaps only leaving behind the ring of stones around a campfire or the folklore surrounding the meaning of a place name. The Sami structures have never been formidable, and our cultural monuments are, above all, memories of culture, transmitted *orally,* as reminders, rather than physical legacies such as a cathedral or a statue.

One of the most prominent Sami cultural figures during the new revitalization from the end of the 1960s was Paulus Utsi (1918-1975). He combined his job as a *duodji*-teacher at the Sami Folk High School in Jokkmokk, Sweden with writing poetry. Utsi had a plan in his writing: he wanted to capture the language, entrap it in the very snares of language itself. He had in mind to write a poetic trilogy, whose individual titles would tell the readers how his plan was progressing. Utsi was able to write two collections before he died, *Giela giela* [Ensnare the lanuage] (1974) and *Giela gielain* [Ensnare with the language] (1980), the second collection appearing posthumously, with his wife, Inger, as co-author. In an interview, Paulus Utsi said that the Sami used to write in the snow, and that made him think of writing poetry. Perhaps it is precisely the transitoriness of this type of writing he had in mind when he, in one of his

11

poems, compares the threatened state of a Sami way of life with ski tracks across the open tundra, which the wind wipes out already before the next morning dawns.

Writing fiction as a creative process, like other cultural work, has, until recently, been something which the Sami have become engaged in more or less reluctantly, not always simply because they have lacked the ability, but often because, in earlier times, no social status was to be gained from that sort of work. It was considered worth knowing how to write, for example in connection with trade and business, but it was mainly the non-Sami who reaped the benefits of their ability to write; and even if the Sami could encourage their children to do well in school in order to do well in the new society, the perception of real work was associated with manual labor and the Biblical edict, "in the sweat of thy brow shalt thou eat thy bread." But Paulus Utsi understood that the Sami also had to learn new techniques, and that, in many ways, they would have to resort to the arts of the non-Sami in order to be heard and taken seriously. Utsi stressed both aspects of writing; its utilitarian value on the one hand – writing as a medium for both learning and livelihood, but also, on the other hand, its esthetic dimension, writing as an art form, as literature, which in its own way can open up completely different avenues for understanding and communication than those which factual prose will ever be able to do. Utsi wanted the Sami to preserve their own language as the minority's own voice, but also to learn the language of the majority in order to expose the majority culture's manipulations of the Sami by means of language; they should become aware of language as a trap with which one could ensnare, but also in which one could be ensnared.

In Sami tradition, anyone who discovers something new must also show that the discovery is significant, viable and of value. Therefore, Paulus Utsi was cautious when he set out to write poetry, first submitting some of his poems for print to the journal *Samefolket,* which is published in Sweden. Next, he wrote a small cycle of poems, made himself heard here and there, gained recognition, became someone from whom people wanted to hear more. And, then, the time was ripe to publish his first collection of poetry, *Giela giela* (Ensnare the language) – that is to say, a call for gaining control over the language. In his second collection, he becomes more explicit about his intentions. It is the language that he wants to capture in the trap, and the weapon he will use, the trap, is language itself, *Giela gielain* (Ensnare with the language), because in Sami, the same words are used for learning languages and checking a trap: *oahppat giela* can mean both "learning a language" and "looking to see if there is anything caught in the trap".

Because of Paulus Utsi's premature death, the trilogy was never completed. Therefore the question is left open and remains unanswered: What might the title of the last volume have been? If he had continued along the same path he had set out, the title of the third volume could have been *Gielain gielain,* which, among other things, can mean "With the language among the languages," in reference to the status of the Sami language as one of many languages in the area where we live. Such a title would, moreover, serve as an appeal that Sami continue to be one of the languages in the North in the future as well; the Sami will have to learn other languages, but also maintain their own.

Proud of the language

What is it, then, that makes the Sami language unique? It is, of course, "the language of the heart" to those for whom it is a mother-tongue, but it is also one of the most developed languages in the world when it comes to describing arctic nature and conditions of life in the North. Sami descriptions of landscape can function as maps, in which are incorporated topography, geography and information as to which routes are best to take. The Sami nomenclature pertaining to snow and reindeer herding is beginning to be recognized internationally. Nils Jernsletten's article describes in more detail these aspects of Sami language from a linguist's point of view. Jernsletten is at the same time a person who himself grew up in the early post-war period knowing – and *using* – these terms in every-day life fishing salmon in the summers and catching ptarmigans in snares in winter to make the ends meet. Sami is a precise language in those areas that demand precision, and, at the same time, it also preserves terms related to kinship, and in so doing, it preserves conceptual knowledge of relationships within and between immediate family and extended kinship.

Sami is a verbal language, both in the sense that it is an oral language and that it, as a vehicle of communication, focuses on the verb, on action. Because it is possible to change a word's meaning and focus by adding an ending to its stem, the language provides possibilities for an almost infinite number of variations. Descriptions of movements may serve as points of illustration. The verb *njuikut,* for instance, means "to jump", without saying anything in particular about how one is jumping. *Njuiket* means "to jump only one time", however, while *njuikkodit* means "to jump continuously." *Njuikestit,* further, means "a small jump, a hop performed once," while *njukkodallat* denotes "several small jumps performed over an extended time". And here one can specify further the nature of the jump itself and the amount of time during which the jump is preformed by saying *njuikulit,* for instance, which can mean both "making a few quick jumps" and "jumping away." *Njuikkodastit* means "to make small jumps for a very short time". *Njuikehit* means "to cause to jump" and "jumping up to get something", but it can also have an entirely different meaning, namely "to copulate", specifically describing how the male animal jumps up on, or mounts, the female during the mating act.

One could continue to add endings to the stem of this verb and create another ten variations or so, but I would rather give another short example, which adds an esthetic dimension to the verb's description of the noun's way of moving. A *beavrrit* is a long-legged, tall and slim human being or animal, in other words, a handsome

14

creature, at least according to today's understanding of what is attractive. From this word one can make verbs like *beavrut, beavrruhit, beavrasaddat* which all describe the special gait or way of moving that this nice-looking human or animal has. A *beavrrit* can be seen in contrast to a *loaggi,* who is a person with short and fat legs, often also dressed in ugly clothes that makes a person look big-butted. The way in which this person moves is described by the words *loaggut* or *loaggahit* (Nielsen 1979: Vol. 1: 306 and Vol. 2: 543).

It is quite obvious that an awareness of the wealth of and possibilities within a person's own language makes him or her proud, and this awareness, therefore, contributes to creating a positive image of the language and the people who use it. The Sami have always been proud of their language, even if the assimilation policies in the Nordic countries during the nineteenth and twentieth centuries reduced the actively Sami-speaking portion of the population considerably (Jernsletten 1993: 122-24). The ambitions regarding one's own mother language are also expressed in the oldest surviving Sami texts describing contacts with other people in the northern regions. The texts were written down in the 1820s, but they refer back to several earlier generations. There the others – the strangers – are referred to as "people without a language," because they don't speak Sami (Fellman 1906: 239-243).

Subordination, resistance and values of our own

Because of the majority culture's political dominance and attempts to assimilate the Sami, and the Sami's gradual subordination, both in terms of their social status and use of their own language, the fundamental relationship between the Sami and the nation states in which they live soon became one of minority and majority. Whereas esthetics, rhetoric and social relationships earlier had been primarily geared toward our own affairs, the political aspect of practically all Sami activities now emerged in the recognition of the Sami's status as a minority. In many cases, being a minority was stigmatized by the assimilationists, something which naturally lay the cornerstone for Sami opposition to being declared incapable of managing their own affairs.

The following essays in this book will implicitly comment on the cultural and political implications of the relationship between majority and minority, for the most part using a Sami point of view on the ways in which research, education and communication serve to shape and promote identity in a modern society. How did the Sami gain control in these three areas, and to what degree have they succeeded in giving them a Sami face? Have they managed to do it, and if so, what is the price they perhaps have had to pay in terms of the power and importance of tradition, a cornerstone in Sami thinking and consciousness? (Seurajärvi-Kari 1995: 82-88, Helander 1996: 1-3, Keskitalo 1994: 51-54).

These questions apply to the management of traditional livelihoods like reindeer herding, as dealt with in Johan K. Hætta Kalstad's article, but equally important is the way today's youth ascribe themselves as Sami without necessarily adopting all the symbols of their parents' generation, as shown in Vigdis Stordahl's essay. The signs and symbols of the 70s have no longer the same meaning in present-day Sami society, even though they were important markers of identity and belonging in the symbolic warfare of the Sami Movement at that time, as Stordahl demonstrates.

In health care the cultural competence of the personnel is important for the success of the treatment, and not least for the trust and confidence of the patients. This self-evident truth still has not been that obvious in regard to the health services previously offered to the Sami, a fact which has been the driving force behind the development of a Sami health care making use of new technical achievements at the same as the cultural background of the patient is taken into consideration. This is relevant at so many levels in the relationship between the treater and the treated, but probably most obvious when it comes to language skills and comprehension of cultural taboos and more or less hidden traditional practices. Health is an important matter for all of us, and the fact that Sami health care so far has been well adjusted to the national health service of Norway should still not be an excuse to leave out a crucial part of the everyday experience of a minority's well-being as presented in Siv Kvernmo's article.

The Sami political awakening was, first and foremost, culturally based. The driving force behind political engagement was directed at insuring the rights to Sami language and culture. Not until later did the issue of rights to land and water come to the fore. The documentation of Sami history, use of Sami as a language in the schools, and news and information services in Sami have always been areas of high priority. Therefore John T. Solbakk's essay in this book on contemporary Sami mass media and their role in shaping a modern Sami society is founded on solid ground when it comes to valuing the importance of having information channels operating in one's own language. Solbakk has his background from media, a fact which is easily traced in his self-experienced account of the recent history of Sami media.

The establishment of Sami institutions of learning was promoted early on as something which would contribute to securing Sami self-awareness and identity. It was important that the Sami themselves be involved and their resources utilized in areas of academic research.[1] The need for Sami researchers became extremely important as a political consideration, both as a disciplinary concern and as a matter of cultural policy. The building-up of a Sami elite and the emphasis on new themes in the ethno-political discourse is thoroughly described in Harald Eidheim's essay on the invention of Sami selfhood. As one of the most influential Norwegian academics supporting the evolving Sami movement and furnishing it with arguments for demanding a greater say in their own affairs, Eidheim's article traces the new Sami self-understanding from the 1970s all the way to the present and illustrates its impact and significance on Sami self determination.

In his article Jan Henry Keskitalo is occupied with the prospects of higher education for a minority people like the Sami. He examines ideals and realities in the endeavors to create academic training adjusted to the cultural background and the needs of the Sami. Being the president (rector) for the first six years of the newly established Sami College in Kautokeino, Keskitalo uses the building-up of this institution as an example of some of the problematics encountered when shaping specifically designed academic programs for relevant minority education in a modern context.

Even if we, in this context, are mainly talking about education according to a Western model, based on studies and theoretical training, we must understand that education as an idea has always held a central position in traditional Sami upbringing. It was important to learn the practical skill, but it was equally important to learn the words and concepts that were associated with the work at hand. This education started early with the stories told by parents and close relatives, stories accompanying concrete work assignments (Vuolab 1995: 33-34). These fictionalized versions of real life were important ingredients in the learning process. Already at a young age, it was important for a child to not only be able to perform a task, but also to explain orally how the task should be carried out; just as it was important to know the terms for landscape and topography in order to be able to describe a geographic location so well to others that they could find it without the use of a map. The great transition that many Sami children experienced when they entered the "Norwegian school" can, I believe, be blamed on the differences between the role of experience in the school setting versus in the Sami children's own world, as well as on the fact that the children were separated from their parents and close relatives and made to live at boarding schools.

A bi-cultural competence

Extending the reasoning I expressed in my description of Paulus Utsi's intended project, one can see that the Sami realized relatively quickly the importance of mastering both their own world and the view that "the others" had of the world. In spite of everything, the Sami have lived in close relationship with their neighbors throughout history, and they have thereby learned that surroundings can be viewed and understood in different ways. Mastering both ways became a strength by itself. While the official Norwegian view on bilingualism has been negative until the last decades, the Sami know better. Our entire history has told us that it is advantageous to master several techniques simultaneously. This was particularly true for the economic basis of Sami life, with combined operations consisting of, for example, farming on a minor scale, sea and lake fishing at different times of the year, berry picking and ptarmigan hunting. Our knowledge is transferable and useful in other contexts, however. Understanding the language of those in power is a precondition for knowing their thoughts; being able to use that language oneself is the most important tool for arguing for a different understanding of the way things are.

Going to Norwegian schools did in fact benefit some Sami children by allowing them to develop a bi-cultural competence – learning Sami values and ideas at home, while at school becoming familiarized with Norwegian history, culture and identity. I am not saying that this applies to all the children – the percentage of "drop-outs" and children who didn't want to or couldn't adjust is too high for that assertion – but it would also be wrong to portray the history of Sami schooling as one of only suffering. Many managed very well in the schools – and still remained Sami. Some of them who have become the most eager advocates of the establishment of a separate Sami school system are themselves products of the school system they call assimilative.[2] An inventory of careers within the Sami society would also most likely confirm that it is exactly those who succeeded in the "Norwegian" school system who have made successful careers. They have solved the dilemma of a person from a minority culture in the modern world – that of having to master the systems of both the majority culture and their own. An interesting remaining question is, however, how do they define their Sami-ness in the modern society? Do they refer to their cultural background and knowledge of tradition as the essence of their "being Sami", or is their newly acquired ethno-political position vis-à-vis the minority and majority societies the main asset of identifying oneself as belonging to both parties?

The minority's other dilemma is, in fact, that, if we want any results whatsoever, we always have to explain our issues in such a way that the powers that be, the majority cultures, understand us. But then there are new potential dangers; when we have learned the language of power, we may begin to forget the thought patterns that form the foundation of our own language. Then our "differentness" can develop into purely a rhetorical veneer, turning us into a kind of political actor without a cultural base. We may ourselves begin to regard experiential knowledge as inferior to scientific knowledge. Science, in the formal sense, has status because it is "rational", while the Sami precise observations and terms are regarded as mere empirical and typological knowledge – and consequently of lesser value. Our perception of the distinction between experiential knowledge and theoretical science has influenced the Sami so much that we have even felt forced to create a new word denoting "science" in order to be on equal footing with the majority culture. The new word *dieda* [science], derived from the verb *diehtit* [to know], is thus set apart from *diehtu* which is the traditional noun for "knowledge".[3]

The terminology for animals and landscape, snow and conditions for traveling on snow, family and kinship is so precise that no scientific system can be more so. Nonetheless, parts of this precise language are in danger of being forgotten because of changes in society and a decreased use of such specialized terms in a modern world where distance between humans – the Sami included – and nature is increasing. An awareness of the fact that, historically, our people have had a scientifically developed language should instill pride in our own language in spite of the fact we, in the past, perhaps haven't differentiated so clearly between knowledge and science. But the differentiation probably was not so important in the past. Do we now have to introduce a separation of the two concepts in order to legitimize Sami research, and, if so, to whom do we legitimize it when we create expressions which perhaps contribute to alienating the user of the language from his or her own linguistic heritage? Will it be possible to operate within two different language-based conceptions of reality and still communicate across these in such a way that people who know the linguistic and cultural codes of both will be able to understand each other?

Are, perhaps, academics, artists and journalists today's architects in the construction of the new Sami society, a society which preserves its own values and traditions while it emphasizes the importance of working within the mainstream in a common effort to learn from and teach each other how to insure the survival of our planet.

The transition from tradition into becoming modern internationalists

One of the aims of this book is to comment on the transition of a traditional culture into the modern way of life – a process we have been witnessing over the last few decades. The changes in societal life, the introduction of state insured welfare programs, the ever increasing amount of consumption, and the dependence on public services has had a tremendous impact on Sami everyday life as well as on the incorporation of the Sami areas into the Norwegian welfare system. This development has been beneficial for the improvement of social conditions in *Sapmi,* the areas where the Sami live, but has, at the same time, contributed to less obvious differences

21

between the Sami way of life and the surrounding Norwegian culture. Being in the state of living in mixed communities over a vast territory, the Sami find themselves making up the majority of the local population only in the inner part of Finnmark, the northenmost county in Norway. In these municipalities there are also certain rights connected with being a Sami. These apply mostly to securing the use of Sami language in public activities. In other areas, like along the coast, the Sami have for a long time been outnumbered by the Norwegian inhabitants, who for the last few hundred years have been in a dominant position.

Some readers may miss a separate essay on the present condition of the land rights's issue in Norway, but for various reasons – and because of the rapid development in the international deliberations on indigenous peoples' rights[4] – the editor decided rather to ask several authors to incorporate those topics into their articles instead of having one essay deal exclusively with legal matters. The material regarding the rights issues is so overwhelmingly huge that a substantial coverage of its full complexity would demand a whole book devoted solely to legal discussions. The intention of this book is rather to elucidate the background and the context for the legal, and political, claims for extended Sami rights – primarily through investigating the cultural foundation for the reasoning behind these demands.

Regarding the historical background for the Sami indigenous rights, I will draw attention to Einar Niemi's essay and his extensive bibliography on the relevant sources examining different aspects of the legitimacy of the Sami claims to land and water rights on the one hand, but where he also deliberates on the problematic situation in Norway concerning these rights, not least with regard to the limited geographical space wherein the separate rights are to be effectuated. Niemi also comments on the situation of the Finnish minority in Norway, the Kven, comparing it to Sami development, and shows the different courses which the political issues of these two groups have had. Niemi presents the current discussions in the wake of the report from the Sami Rights' Commission, NOU 1997:4. This report which deals with land management in Finnmark, the northernmost county of Norway, states that land rights should not be granted on a specific ethnic basis. Implicit in this principle is the obligation of the Norwegian authorities to secure the preservation and development of Sami culture in Norway. This means that rights have a cultural, not an ethnic basis, and that it is out of respect for the cultural persistence which in turn implements growth and development in local societies that the national authorities accept specific rights granted to the habitants of particular regions. These prerogatives are not based in individual rights of a specific ethnic group, but as a means of securing the continued existence of Sami culture collectively.

According to the Commission, it is necessary to make certain exceptions and to grant special rights to the Sami in order to achieve equity between Norwegian and Sami culture in Norway. The same kind of logic is the foundation for the suggestion that local management of specific resources within defined limited areas be safeguarded as the natural basis for Sami culture. As a consequence of this thinking, and in the wording of the Commission to avoid local dissension, different models of natural resource management are proposed with equal representation by Sami and Norwegians elected by the Sami Parliament and the Finnmark County Parliament. The Commission refuses rights based on ethnic criteria out of practical reasons connected with difficulties in management, and because of disadvantageous consequences – not on the basis of a principal view.

Most of the contributors in this collection are Sami themselves, and therefore occupied in issues of how to shape and reshape the values of the past into a future that will still be recognized as values belonging to "natural man". Defending an indigenous peoples' culture in a modern world must mean something in practice for the Sami both collectively and individually. There must be some cognitive and even philosophical justification for maintaining and developing a culture and a world-view which for "modern man" may seem outdated and backward. Even though the Sami probably are one of the most modernized indigenous peoples in the world, their role as communicators between an ever more estranged "Western" conception of Nature and the indigenous peoples' preferred holistic view expressing the statement that all creatures are fundamentally dependent on each other, is important and steadily growing. This is the time to utilize the benefits of belonging to the affluent countries of the world, and also to benefit from a modern education system that enables the Sami of today to assume the position of mediators: advocating the view of the "natural man" to the international society of the UN and the IMF, and, at the same time, convincing the indigenous peoples about the importance of letting one's voice be heard by the international community. This is the task and the challenge of modern natural man, still hearing and obeying the heartbeats of the Earth itself, imparting its message through the most modern mediums to an increasing number of serious listeners.

One of the intended, or at least, hoped for distinctive qualities of this book is the devotedness to a cause manifested by every writer. The contributors are not just outside observers to events and tendencies, they are, on the contrary, deeply involved with the issues at hand. They analyze ongoing processes at the same time as they themselves take part in shaping the future society by being active members of the community. Their involvement and their enthusiasm is the strength of this book – the development and achievements described are to some extent the products of the strivings of the same people. The present collection of articles should be the best proof for my assertion in this introduction that the Sami want to have a say in the shaping of the future society as well as in the research conducted on our own culture, history and management of land as well as identity and belonging to a place and a people.

The tribal voice in the new political discourse

In opposition to this goal is the awareness that this boundary between a Western course of action and that taken by the indigenous peoples are erased in the everyday world of Sami politics, because political interactions are becoming identical all over the world. There is only one way to speak on the international arena if a person wants to be heard and understood. Therefore, the representatives of the indigenous peoples who are expected to act as intermediaries between different world views need to have tremendous communication skills; the destiny of the indigenous peoples depends on how well Western society understands them and how interested in them it is, but the survival of Western society is perhaps also dependent on its gaining a new understanding of "the first voices". Because the discourse of politics is becoming increasingly "tainted", it is necessary to turn to the art of the indigenous peoples and to tradition to rediscover the central questions regarding our existence on earth. Whereas the politicians among the indigenous peoples nowadays speak with "the White Man's Voice", it is perhaps still possible to hear "the Tribal Voice"[5] resonate in indigenous art, both in traditional art and in the modern interpretations of, for example, what it means to be a Sami today.

Therefore, both art and science are in the process of revitalizing their roles as identity markers for many indigenous peoples of the world. Both disciplines defy limits and borders, also in an ethnic sense, and, therefore, they provide the best point of departure for the establishment and continuation of contact between different people and nations. One conspicuous Sami example of art work in this line are the books by the award-winning poet Nils-Aslak Valkeapää. On the cover of his book, *The Sun, My Father* Valkeapää has the image of a golden magical drum. In the middle of the drum, he places the Sami sun symbol, which also appears in the book together with a creation story, told in the form of a poem. Among the photographs included in the book are those of Sami mythological places

25

and old, preserved drums. Toward the end of the book Valkeapää returns to images of the drum but now it is torn.

The poems at the end of the book revolve around the concept of time, and the form of one of the poems is also a semi-circle that declares:"and time does not exist, no end, none/ and time is, eternal, always, is..." (poem no. 566). Completing a circle, the book's first poem is repeated at the end, not in completely identical form, but with the same theme. When the words come to an end, we carry with us the last poem of the book:"...and when everything is over/nothing is heard any more/ nothing/and it is heard." (no. 570). When we close the book, we discover that the back cover doesn't have the entire drum, only the figure of the sun which we found positioned in the center of the drum on the front cover. Time has changed, old beliefs disappear, but the knowledge imparted by the traditions that the Sami pay heed to is, among other things, the awareness that we are descendants of the Sun with all the obligations attached to that in terms of how we live today: as an indigenous people in more than a political sense.

1   Cf. the discussion about locating the first Sami Institute of Research outside of the newly founded University of Tromsø that took place when the Nordic Sami Institute was created in Kautokeino in 1974. Some of the arguments for a separate establishment in the geographic center of the Sami settlements can be found in A. I. Keskitalo 1976. In 1989 a Sami College was established in the same village.

2   See also Stordahl's article in this book. Otherwise there has been a great deal of research and writing about how the Norwegian (and Swedish and Finnish) school has not worked vis-à-vis Sami children and Sami traditions. This is partly connected with research done about the period of "Norwegianization" of the Sami and of the Finnish immigrants, and the formation of boarding schools which were part of the strategy to "Norwegianize" Sami children. Sources on these topics include Asle Høgmo 1989, Anton Hoëm 1976, L. Lind Meløy 1980, and Knut Einar Eriksen and Einar Niemi 1981. Among more recent material on the position of the school within today's Sami

society, attention must de drawn to a booklet named *Kunnskap og kompetanse i Sápmi "En samisk skole i emning"* [Knowledge and Competence in Sapmi: The development of a Sami School] (ed. A. Balto), SUFUR 1996, where the current system is evaluated and different approaches tried out regarding new ways to develop an education more in harmony with Sami values and traditions.

3   Cf. K Nielsen's dictionary in which the concept of "dieđa" is not included. The main part of Nielsen's dictionaries were compiled from the beginning of the the twentieth century up to the beginning of WWII. In Pekka Sammalahti's *Sámi-Suoma sátnegirji*, 1989:110, the concept is included meaning 'science'.

4   See more on the international movement of indigenous peoples, and their role in foregrounding the land rights' issue in international fora as the UN in H. Minde 1996, especially 242-44 where he gets into the background for establishing a separate Working Group on Indigenous Population (WGIP or UN working group) in 1982.

5   This expression is borrowed from the CD by the aboriginal Australian group, Yotho Yindi. The title of the CD is *The Tribal Voice Album* (Mushroom Records, Australia, 1991).

References:

Balto, Asta. (ed.) 1996. *Kunnskap og kompetanse i Sápmi. "En samisk skole i emning",* Kunnskapsbilder, Forskningsserie fra SUFUR. Karasjok, Davvi Girji OS.

Eriksen, Knut Einar and Einar Niemi. 1981. *Den finske fare: Sikkerhetsproblemer og minoritetspolitikk i nord 1860-1940,* Oslo, Universitetsforlaget.

Fellman, Jacob. 1906. *Anteckningar under min vistelse i Lappmarken* II, Helsingfors: 239-243.

Gaski, Harald. 1993. "The Sami People: The 'White Indians' of Scandinavia." *American Indian Culture and Research Journal,* Vol. 17, No. 1: 115-128. Los Angeles, UCLA.

Guttorm, Gunvor. 1995. "Duodji / Sami Handicrafts – A Part of the Whole", *On the Terms of Northern Women,* Tuohimaa S. et al. (eds.), Northern Gender Studies Publication Series, No. 1, Oulu, Femina Borealis.

Helander, Elina. 1996. "Sustainability in the Sami area: The X-file factor", *Awakened Voice. The Return of Sami Knowledge,* Helander, E. (ed.), Guovdageaidnu, Nordic Sami Institute, *Diedut,* Vol. 4: 1-6.

Hoëm, Anton. 1976. *Makt og kunnskap,* Oslo, Universitetsforlaget.

Høgmo, Asle. 1989. *Norske idealer og samisk virkelighet; om skoleutvikling i det samiske området,* Oslo, Gyldendal.

Jernsletten. Nils. 1993. "Sami language communities and the conflict between Sami and Norwegian", *Language Conflict and Language Planning,* Jahr, E.H. (ed.), Berlin-New York, Mouton de Gruyter: 115-132.

Keskitalo, A.I. 1976. Research As An Inter-Ethnic Relation, *Acta Borealis* B. Humaniora No. 13: 15-42.

Keskitalo, J.H. 1994. "Education and Cultural Policies", *Majority – Minority Relations. The Case of the Sami in Scandinavia.* Report. *Diedut* No. 1, Guovdageaidnu, Sámi Instituhtta.

Meløy, L. Lind. 1980. *Internatliv i Finnmark. Skolepolitikk 1900-1940,* Oslo, Det Norske Samlaget.

Minde, Henry. 1996. "The Making of an International Movement of Indigenous Peoples", *Scandinavian Journal of History,* Vol. 21, No. 3: 221-246.

Nielsen, Konrad. 1979. *Lappisk (Samisk) ordbok I-V,* Oslo, Institutt for sammenlignenede kulturforskning.

NOU 1997: 4. *Naturgrunnlaget for samisk kultur.*

Sammalahti, Pekka. 1989. *Sámi-Suoma sátnegirji,* Ohcejohka, Jorgaleaddji Oy.

Seurajärvi-Kari, Irja. 1995. "Indigenous Women in the Changing World", *On the Terms of Northern Women,* Tuohimaa S. et al. (eds.), Northern Gender Studies Publication Series, No. 1, Oulu, Femina Borealis: 83-88.

Valkeapää, Nils-Aslak. 1989. *Beaivi, Áhčážan,* Kautokeino, DAT.

Valkeapää, Nils-Aslak. 1997. *The Sun, My Father.* Kautokeino, DAT, (Distribution in North America by the University of Washington Press, Seattle).

Vuolab, Kerttu. 1995. "Riggodagaid botnihis gáldu – máidnasiid mearihis mearkkašupmi", *cafe Boddu 2,* Gaski, H and J.T. Solbakk (eds.) [a collection of essays in Sami], Karasjok, Davvi Girji OS: 23-35.

Yotho Yindi. 1991. *The Tribal Voice Album,* Mushroom Records.

Harald Eidheim

Ethno-Political Development among the Sami after World War II

The Invention of Selfhood[1]

The Sami world has, during the latter half of the twentieth century, undergone a revolutionary development. At the end of the Second World War, life conditions for the Sami may briefly be summarized as follows:

As a numerically small population of about 40-50 thousand people living on the sub-arctic outskirts of Europe and spread as minorities in four countries - Finland, Norway, Russia and Sweden, the Sami lacked a unifying socio-political organization. In this scattered population there were significant regional differences, both with regard to language and culture. Their knowledge of each other was specific to individual localities. This meant that, among other things, most Samis' knowledge of Sami in regions other than their own was either very nearly absent and/or of an anecdotal character.

When considering this state of affairs, it may seem surprising that this dispersed Sami population during the course of only a few decades gradually developed a collective self-understanding, a unifying communications network and an ethno-political fellowship. This was also manifested through a flowering cultural creativity (Eidheim 1992).

There are several factors to consider when attempting to describe and explain this development. First and foremost, we have to consider what has been the very driving force in this development, namely the ethno-political movement which gained a permanent foothold among the Sami populace around the middle of the century. This movement has both inspired the development of a new Sami collective self-understanding and it has participated in the political organization of the Sami, and, with considerable success,

29

it has fought for Sami rights – and the freedom to live as an independent people.

The movement arose at the initiative of a handful of Sami in the Nordic countries. In recent years, the Sami population of the Kola peninsula in Russia has also been able to ally itself with the Sami Movement's vision of a more powerful cultural self-assertion and a future in which the Sami can govern their own destiny. Gradually, and to a greater and greater degree, the Sami Movement has activated the majority of the Sami population.

The emergent collective self-understanding also has resulted in the Sami viewing themselves in a larger perspective. They have developed strong bonds of solidarity with indigenous populations of other parts of the world and have, in a more general perspective, positioned themselves as a people, as a nation in inter-cultural global space.

This article is an attempt to sketch out some developmental lines and cast light on certain contexts with the aim of presenting a simplified but comprehensive picture of the cultural and political development of the Sami during this period of time. The theoretical and ethno-political perspective which is utilized has been culled from the literature of social anthropology (cf., e.g. Barth 1969, 1994; Dyck 1985; Eidheim 1971, 1992; Paine 1984, 1985; Wagner 1981).

It is important, right at the start, to take into consideration what it means to say that the Sami live as an ethnic minority in the countries exercising sovereignty over Sapmi – the land of the Sami. In the three Nordic countries, the position of Sami as ethnic minorities has many similarities, while there are more distinctive differences between these on the one hand and the conditions which prevail between the Sami and the state in Russia. To illustrate what a minority position implies, I shall briefly and generally summarize some of the main elements of the Sami minority position in Norway at the time when they started to organize after the Second World War.

The Domination of the majority

The relation between the minority and the majority populace/state is characterized by the fact that the Sami live inside a state created and governed by Norwegians. History reveals how it came about that the state demanded and enforced sovereignty over areas long inhabited and used by the Sami, areas which the Sami consider their homeland. It also reveals how the state, in legal terms, has not distinguished between Sami and Norwegians. The Norwegian people have stood behind this process of state creation, which must be seen as an expression of the Norwegian people's self-assertion vis-á-vis other states and peoples. This created an asymmetrical relationship between the people that had created and maintained a state in order to ensure and secure their self-determination and their basic cultural values on the one hand, and the Sami population on the other, which, in this same process, was deprived of its right to self-determination.

This means that the Sami population was not recognized as a rights-holding entity within the state system. Having no rights in or to their homeland, they were not given the same opportunities to cultivate and develop their language and their culture as a minority population. In this respect, the Sami in each of the four countries lived under the dominance and authority of another people, while their culture was threatened with extinction.

Infrequent and short-lived attempts to organize the Sami, and a cautious formulation of demands for Sami rights took place already in the beginning of the 20th century (Jernsletten 1986), but it was not until after the Second World War that this attempt at organization became a permanent and politically significant phenomenon. This was a time when humanist ideals concerning human and political rights of ethnic minorities were the focus of greater attention at the international level, and the Scandinavian countries were among those who desired to become the advocates of new and more liberal principles and regulations in this area. This created greater oppor-

31

tunities for "Sami self-organising initiatives" than had previously existed in the Nordic countries. From the fragmented Sami population, a small elite emerged during the 50s which began to build up an organized and unifying ethno-political people's movement. It has, since the 60s, been called the "Sami Movement" (Eidheim 1971). This awakening implies that the Sami gradually reevaluated their self-image, invented a new context for a unifying, cultural commonality, and, step by step, became a political force on the Nordic scene.

In a cultural-political perspective, this development may be viewed as the invention of a new paradigm for Sami self-understanding. The cognitive aspect of this process has taken the form of a recodification of Sami history, culture and distinctiveness – what we may call the identification of a "common cultural estate." The political aspect has taken the form of attempts to cement a new and politically motivating self-understanding among the Sami, and a mobilization of the Sami behind demands for specific rights for the Sami as a people: recognition and maintenance of Sami language, culture and territorial rights.

This awakening, which, on the level of the individual also signified a new experience of ethnic pride, fellowship and spirit, also implied the dissemination throughout the population of a clearer perception of the Samis' relationship to the majority population and to the state. That is, a new perception of the Sami inter-cultural relationships, which had been traditionally characterised by powerlessness, cultural stigma, and feelings of inferiority and ethno-political apathy, was forged. The feeling of powerlessness in relation to the state power and the majority culture had, however, left deep scars in the population, and the message broadcast by the elite met with no immediate success. In fact, the process of gaining support on the part of the Sami proceeded at a slow pace. Many Sami were of the opinion that this public and self-appointed way of expressing oneself about Sami fellowship was un-Sami both in thought and action.

The people who emerged as spokesmen for these new ideas were perceived by many as romanticists and rabble rousers, mostly interested in attracting attention to themselves. Many Sami expressed publicly the belief that assimilation into the majority culture was the most realistic alternative. The reaction of the Norwegian authorities to the argument that the Sami had a right to reforms by virtue of being a people was that these elite persons were far from representing Sami opinion. In addition, it was frequently pointed out that the Sami enjoyed uncurtailed rights as Norwegian citizens. The attitude of the authorities was also that if there could be found deficiencies of an either economic or welfare nature in the Sami areas, then these could be made good by means of regional subsidies and measures. It was proposed, for example, to implement measures which provided Sami-speaking children and youth in Sami-speaking districts better Norwegian language skills to rectify their typically disadvantaged status vis-à-vis welfare benefits.

Nevertheless, the picture the elite painted of the Sami situation could not, in the long run, be dismissed. If the state's self-proclaimed adherence to the ideals of human rights, and in particular, minority rights, were to be taken seriously, reforms had to be implemented. In their movement, the Sami elite were to experience the suspicion and contempt of many other Sami, and yet, they could also take credit for significant progress in advancing the Sami political cause.

A new Sami self-understanding

When reviewing this immediate history from the vantage point of the 1990s in order to explain the development which has taken place, it is necessary to emphasize certain important, trend-setting historical events, and to indicate how some general cognitive and culturally new orientations have gained a foothold and grown in the Sami population. The new Sami self-understanding which spread slowly among the population from the 1960s onwards shows that the Sami identity is experienced by more and more people – not only as a contrasting identity to the minority's majority counterpart, the *Dáža* [a Sami word, meaning any non-Sami] but, at the same time, as a complementary identity which creates the possibility of experiencing equality vis-à-vis the same counterpart.

We have already touched on the most important historical event, namely that the Sami Movement gained a foothold and an institutional basis. The visible, public manifestation of this was that the Sami elite established active and viable voluntary organizations among the Sami in the Nordic countries and that a common Nordic umbrella organization, the Nordic Sami Council, was established in 1956. These organizations were important instruments in the mobilization of ethno-politically active Sami and they channeled Sami views and demands to the authorities in the Nordic countries.

During the first years the core elite in the Sami Movement played a key role in this development. They used the Sami language, culture and history to give substance to the idea that the Sami possessed something valuable and honourable to take care of – a heritage which was taken from them and which had to be recaptured. The Sami elite, equipped with the knowledge of state organization, argued that the Sami had been dispossessed of the possibility to develop as an people, and were virtual illiterates in their own language as a result of being forced into a school system designed to promote competence in Norwegian, and thus were denied access to cultural competency. They here touched on feelings of inferiority deeply ingrained in most Sami as a painful complex of shame, self-contempt and unreleased aggression (Fokstad 1966).

In this intermediary role that the elite thus assumed, they argued, based on a knowledge of international human rights discussions, and, in particular those concerning indigenous peoples' freedoms and rights, that equality for the Sami would have to be based on their being a unique and individual people. Based on this status, then, that the Sami be granted specific rights and given real opportunities to develop their own culture economically and organizationally, alongside their language and their society. In accordance with this, they presented arguments for certain legal changes, for a new educational policy which would harmonize with the ideals of equality, for measures and allocations which could increase the general standard of living in the Sami districts, and for the Sami right to land and water in the traditional Sami areas.

In the cultural invention which the Sami Movement thus instigated, a pattern emerges already in the 60s. The movement acquired its power of conviction and growing ethno-political strength through the appropriation and conventionalizing of new knowledge of a Sami cultural heritage and through growing awareness, on the part of an increasing number of Sami, of the relationship with the outside world. In the organization of this knowledge, the idea that the Sami are a people is the central tenet. The incipient self-understanding was not only based upon a discovery and a new evaluation of the Sami past and cultural heritage, it was also nourished by the fact that the Sami Movement – to the surprise of many – reaped political gains by the manner in which they presented their case.

The data reveal that the allocations made by the Norwegian state in response to the Sami Movement, increased from the 1960s and onwards: funds went into the training of Sami teachers, Sami language education at teacher colleges and universities, the development of Sami media, Sami handicraft production, and, significantly, in support of the organizational work of the Sami Movement. It is important to note that the support from the state in this phase was not based on any admission that the Sami had rights as a people. It was given with reference to a welfare ideology and to general welfare criteria. The Sami Movement, on the other hand, could transform this into an expression of political gains which strengthened its ethno-political project.

All these new events and tendencies which could be converted into new knowledge and new arguments, gave inspiration to a more and more extended discourse on what it meant to be a Sami (Stordahl 1996). This discourse showed that there were various opinions in the population with regard to the degree to which one should present oneself ethno-politically – if at all – in the way encouraged by the Sami Movement. Additionally, there were divergent opinions even within the movement itself about the way in which the relationship of the Sami to the state and to the majority population should be redesigned.

New themes in the ethno-political discourse

The politically active – the organizers and main driving force behind the Sami Movement – for quite some time numbered only a few dozen people, but it is symptomatic of this process of historical development that the discourse they inspired gradually activated the large majority of the Sami populace during the course of the 70s and 80s. A new and significant theme in this discourse arose in that the leadership of the Sami Movement established permanent contact with indigenous peoples' organizations in other parts of the world. The Sami Movement, through the auspices of the Nordic Sami Council, participated in the establishment of the World Council of Indigenous Peoples (WCIP) in 1975, and Sami representatives have since carried out significant work in this organization.

The spread of an awareness of a shared destiny and common interests knowledge about what it meant to belong to an indigenous people and that they could share a common destiny and common interests with comparable peoples in distant lands planted the seeds of a new and more global dimension in the discourse on the significance of being a Sami. No longer was the ethno-political battle fought in the context of the Sami against the state powers of the three Nordic countries. To a greater and greater extent, the Sami viewed themselves as participants in a greater global movement of indigenous peoples which fought for their rights and their cultural survival as peoples on the international arena – in the corridors of the UN and at the Commission for Human Rights in Geneva.

The intensification of Sami involvement in inter-cultural affairs was manifested in several ways; participation in world-wide indigenous peoples' conferences and festivals, and in the Nordic Sami Council hosting WCIP world conferences. This international circulation of people, value orientations and symbols resulted in increased significance at the local level of argumentation and organization in the Sami area. The status of the Sami as an indigenous people was now more and more brought into play in local issues. This could apply to educational issues concerning local schools, the construction of Sami day care centers, or concrete concessional issues involving the bonding of land areas or other encroachments upon the natural environment which were perceived as harmful to Sami enterprise, and thereby, to the survival of Sami culture. And it also concerned, of course, the constantly present and controversial questions of the Sami "right to land and water" and their "right to self-determination." In sum, throughout the 1970s and 80s, it became increasingly common for ordinary Sami people to view their existence and cultural survival in terms of *an indigenous peoples' perspective;* a tendency which accentuates what we might call the prelude to an *aboriginalization* of Sami ethno-politics and self-understanding.

The indigenous people's perspective was, in a dramatic way, made relevant in the well known Alta affair (to which I shall return below), a controversial issue over the construction of a dam on the Alta-Kautokeino watercourse (Brantenberg 1985, Paine 1982). Firstly, however, we need to look at some important contextual changes which originated independently of the Sami Movement, but which became extremely consequential for the cultural invention of Sami selfhood.

We have already seen how one of them, the international development in human rights, became a stepping stone for the Sami Movement. Two other and very fundamental factors which also must be taken into consideration are a considerable rise of the educational standards in the population and the establishment of the modern welfare state and rising standard of living in Sami society.

Education

During the period of rebuilding in Norway which followed in the wake of WW II it became increasingly obvious that the standard of living in the Sami areas, especially those areas in the north where the Sami population was most densely concentrated, lagged far behind the rest of the country. This was evident with reference to economy as well as education and health. Raising the standard of education among the Sami by establishing a fully adequate general education based on the Sami language and culture was a matter of principal concern in the Sami Movement's reform policies. This was not conceived first and foremost as an instrument with which to raise the material standard of living. More fundamentally, it was perceived as a goal in itself to spread general knowledge and professional skills which could further the establishment of a cultural and ethno-political self-consciousness. As far as this ambition was concerned, the introduction in Norway of a nine-year compulsory educational system in the 1960s was of great significance.

The teaching of the Sami language was first introduced into the debate on education as a purely pedagogical issue. Some voices were heard suggesting that it would benefit the learning of Norwegian if one already possessed elementary knowledge of one's Sami mother tongue. The training of teachers able to teach Sami at the elementary school level started gradually, and several projects in teaching Sami at elementary schools were begun in a few municipalities. The educational reforms which the Sami Movement favored received support from researchers and other experts, and the authorities gradually began to accept that the Sami had a right to instruction in their own language. The profound value which the concept of the mother tongue has in Norwegian culture created an atmosphere in which general Norwegian opinion lent a sympathetic ear to the Sami Movement's arguments, and reforms were gradually put into practice: a Sami grammar school, language and culture training at some teacher training colleges, advanced education in

Sami language and culture at the university level, and special provisions which created opportunities for educating more Sami in various professions (on the assumption that more Sami could then be recruited to occupations in the Sami districts which demanded higher education but which had historically been filled by Norwegians). Considering the meager conditions which had prevailed, the 60s heralded a veritable explosion in the higher education of the Sami population during the 70s and 80s. Many of those who received an education returned to the Sami districts and filled positions previously not open to Sami on the basis of education in health care, education, social work, engineering and in the newly emerging Sami media.

Education also proved to be a means to ethnic self-understanding that was in line with the perspective of the pioneers. Education attracted many younger Sami-speaking professionals into the Sami Movement. There they became active in the work of recodification and advancing Sami ethno-politics vis-à-vis the state powers as well as throughout the extended global space. From having trailed far behind the country's average up to the 60s as regards the advanced education of young people, there are signs which indicate that the Sami districts by 1990 have reached the level of the national average. On the other hand, the process of reorganizing teaching plans at lower and middle levels of general education towards a system based wholly on the Sami language and culture has proceeded much more slowly. There is still much to do in this field. Nonetheless, viewed as a whole, there has been a considerable increase in literacy in Sami language and culture, a fact which has induced an intensification of the discourses surrounding tradition and renewal, and, thereby, around the themes which reflect the modern Samis self-understanding and collective life expression. These discourses take place not only in peoples' everyday life, in the kitchens and reindeer herdsmen's tents, in cafés and at more formal gatherings, they are also observable in new Sami literature, on the theatre stage, in television programs, in popular music and in Sami art and handicrafts (Gaup

1982, Gaski 1988, NRK Sámi Radio 1990, Persen 1989, Rajala 1990, Henriksen & Johnskareng 1976, Fossbakk 1987).

Affluence and consumption

During the 1960s and 1970s a third factor emerged, independent of the Sami Movement, which had complex and fundamental consequences for the Sami population and for the development of a modern Sami culture. This was the general increase in employment figures and living standards in Norway. The country as a whole experienced a positive economic development, and, in the northernmost counties, the rebuilding after WW II was complete and full employment reigned. The reconstruction of a commercialized and technologically contemporary agriculture developed apace with the reconstruction of fisheries and associated industries, with the commercialization and technologizing of the reindeer industry, and changed the conditions of life in Sami areas. The development of a transportation network, roads, electrical service, and, not least, the introduction of snowmobiles and private cars had an almost revolutionary significance for communications and the standard of living in an area of great distances and tiny, remote population centers.

The improvement of the welfare and health care systems, in addition to improving the standard of living in remoter areas of the country, created many new and relatively well paying jobs in the Sami districts, especially in civil service, health and social services, and education. During the 1950s, the percentage of the Sami population which was employed in the primary industries of reindeer pastoralism, agriculture and the fisheries, and which combined various additional income sources such as hunting, berry gathering, etc., thus decreased drastically, whereas the percentage of wage workers, especially in the service industry, increased (Stordahl 1996).

This development resulted in people in the entire Sami area acquiring improved private economies which were apparently administered in ways that did not deviate in any significant degree from what we might call the model of the Scandinavian middle class. Those who built new houses during this period invested, for the most part, in tip-top, modern, detached houses. Others installed bathrooms and toilets, built extensions and effectively insulated their houses against the winter cold. People used money on modern kitchen technology and furniture for their sitting rooms and lounges, and radios and televisions could be found in everybody's homes. The enjoyment of leisure time and holidays now became an important element of peoples' consumption patterns. More and more built huts and chalets in the country for weekend and holiday use, and spent money on modern sports equipment for hunting and fishing. A growing number of people saved money in order to be able to spend summer holidays further afield, e.g. on the Swedish shores of the Gulf of Bothnia, in one or another of the big cities of Europe or on a sunny beach of some Mediterranean island. Educational loans and stipends were made more easily accessible. The state and municipalities financed the building of modern schools (the old boarding school system was abolished). Swimming halls, modern sport centres, retirement and nursing homes, and Sami day care centers were built in population centres.

The collectivization of new knowledge, conceptions and images

It goes without saying that these general developments in education and knowledge, and in welfare and consumption, combined with the increasing identification of the Sami with the notion of being an "indigenous people" marked a discernible shift in life styles and in notions of what it meant to be Sami. Analytically speaking, we may say that people came to handle a larger and larger repertory of new and strange sign material, something which had the effect of intensifying the discourse concerning what it meant to be a Sami. The rather obvious question which arises from this development is, of

41

course, how it was possible to adopt and collectivize new and radically alien elements and, at the same time, objectivize and renew the experience of a community which is Sami.

There is no simple and final answer to this question – but I would like to draw attention to one important aspect, i.e. that the appropriation of an ethnic collective identity, selfhood or peoplehood, implies a collectivization of conceptions and images which makes it possible continually to reinvent this selfhood in a more and more complex life-world. This can clearly be read out of the revitalization process as it gained ground during the 70s and 80s. Not only the elite, but a wider range of Sami society, including the younger generation and those with higher education, built up a repertory of knowledge and concepts and symbols by means of which this new spirit and self-understanding was perceived and communicated (Johnsen 1972, Utsi 1976). In addition to the heightened public awareness of belonging to a "people," a growing sector of the Sami population also learned to perceive and use the expression "our culture" and "the Sami culture" as notions indicating Sami ways of life. They learned to perceive and to identify with a synthesis of Sami livelihoods, languages and folkways to communicate a wide range of meanings and feelings. Prominent among these was the newly formed concept of their history as a people who had established their homeland on the tundra, the coasts and the woodlands in the north long before the Nordic people arrived on the scene. This new Sami culture also emphasized Sami achievements in modern times, i.e. the ethno-political mobilization in educational standards and renewed artistic creativity.

In the Sami ethno-political discourse a number of other concepts and expressions also gained a foothold, e.g. "Sami identity," "our identity," and even "ethnicity" and "Sami ethnicity." Also the colonialist aspect of the relationship between the state and the Sami people was substantiated and fitted into the groundwork of this new self-understanding. In the central Sami areas, Sami youngsters could now learn about the Sami past and to read and write their mother tongue at school. Sami authors wrote on Sami history and several local museums were established to conserve local variants of their cultural heritage (Aikio 1980, Jernsletten et al. 1983). In this sense, the appropriation of Sami selfhood and application of the concept of modern "nationhood" was accomplished through the invention of new historical emblems. This is *inter alia* also conspicuously signalled by a flowering handicraft industry based on, and inspired by, traditional prototypes.

The 70s and 80s also witnessed the establishment of new Sami professional organizations. Up to this time only the reindeer pastoralists had had their own organization. Now, a number of additional new Sami professional associations came into being and attracted considerable attention and surprise: associations for teachers, social workers, artists, doctors, sports, women, and a touring Sami theatre came into permanent function. Activities and arrangements prefixed with "Sami-" flourished: festivals of various kinds, sport events, exhibitions, and, of course, seminars on political, cultural and professional issues. The Sami Research Institute was established in the early 70s and a Sami college in the late 80s in Kautokeino, in the Sami heartland.

As a result of Sami ethno-political pressure, such initiatives were mostly financed by the state or by official funds. Thus, the importance and authority of the Sami Movement as an ethno-political force became more and more evident as it continued to capture the attention of the general public with arguments for equality and pleas for greater Sami self-determination.

Bonds of solidarity between the Sami "nation" and other indigenous peoples were strengthened. It became increasingly common for visitors from far-away continents to tour Sami areas, taking part in Sami public events of various kinds and exchanging information and views with Sami people. Likewise, Sami representatives, now equipped with travel funds, foreign language competencies, and various professional skills, travelled widely and further developed relations with the "Fourth World." As partners in discussions and as consultants, Sami delegates have joined delegates from other indigenous peoples' in international forums devoted to the codification of principles for the protection of indigenous peoples' rights and freedoms.

Particularly significant for the expression of selfhood was the revival of the name Sapmi, a concept indicating the "Sami world" of land and waters, people and culture. It was quickly elevated to a new and extended validity and dignity (Stordahl 1996). Deep-seated emotional and even non-communicable aspects of being a Sami and of belonging to a homeland as well as notions of the factual aspects of Sami history and culture could readily be imputed to it. A Sami artist prepared a map of Sapmi (omitting the national borders criss crossing the area) in which he, by means of a thousand place names, indicated Sami geographical and cultural space (Mathisen 1982). A Sami flag was also designed and was quickly adopted and brought into use throughout Sapmi in various forms such as badges and stickers on school satchels, bags, cars and snowmobiles, etc. The "Sami colours" used in the flag (medium blue, red, green and yellow – the most common colours in traditional Sami national costumes) also spread throughout Sapmi and some official buildings were even painted in these colours indoors. The press and television took note of these forms of self-expression and symbols and reflected them back in news coverage, commentaries, documentaries and feature programmes broadcast in the Sami language. The Sami, of course, also presented themselves at inter-cultural events by means of these symbols.

There was, after 1970, also a "flowering" of new Sami literature, art and sculpture, many works winning recognition and fame far from home (Gaski 1991, Birktvedt 1991, Rajala 1990). There was also an increased interest in the traditional Sami yoik as well as in new songs and popular melodies with texts inspired by the new era in Sapmi. This new pop music, played by Sami groups, also added a characteristic tone to the invention of a new Sami youth culture (Dædnugadde nuorat 1974, Henriksen & Johnskareng 1976).

In that part of the Sami population which was strongly affected by stigmatization and assimilation – such as the coastal Sami population – people started to perceive the contours of a new epoch. Even though their cultural competence as Sami was slight, – perhaps they could not even speak Sami – some of them, nonetheless, saw the possibility of obtaining a variant of this new and modern way of adaptation to life as Sami. In many such hamlets there were people who now more conspicuously identified themselves as Sami and gave their support to the Sami Movement even though they also had to experience being judged as second-rate Sami by some of the younger ethno-political "lions."

The conspicuous growth of these new characteristics of Sami self-representation – the vocabulary, the new-found competence and self-confidence in presenting the Sami ethno-political situation as part of a world-wide phenomenon, the cultural self-expression and development – all attracted attention. This occurred first in the Nordic countries, but soon was seen further afield. The mass media of the Nordic countries, which had previously tended to ignore the Sami Movement, started to become interested in the ethno-political signals from this quarter and references in the media to the Sami situation increased during the 70s and 80s.

The Alta affair – an event in inter-cultural space

The invention of a new Sami self-understanding and the idioms and orientations through which it is conveyed can be seen as the result of events of extreme complexity and range; from the level of the family and the local, to the pan-Sami and global level. The Alta affair was, in this respect, a mega-happening which accentuated all the vital aspects of the Sami situation as a *people*, as *an ethnic minority population* in Norway, and as an indigenous people in a global perspective.

If we survey the background for the Alta affair we may note the following: as the Sami Movement increased in strength and attracted attention during the 60s and 70s, a pattern became established in what we might term "the dialogue" between the Sami Movement and the Norwegian State (Eidheim, 1985). When the Sami Movement argued for reforms from a position located in the ideal of equality between cultures and ethnic groups and with a basis in fundamental Sami rights as a people and an indigenous population, they were met with answers which were based on the rights and obligations of the Sami as citizens of Norway. This stressed more and more clearly the disparity which existed between the country's international involvement in efforts to create support for principles of recognition and protection of ethnic minorities and indigenous peoples' freedoms and rights, and the lack of recognition of such freedoms and rights when it came to the Sami within the country's own boundaries.

In the course of this dialogue between the state and the Sami Movement, the state constantly supplied new material for which the Sami Movement found use in their work, clarifying and substantiating their message not only internally among the Sami population but also vis-à-vis the state and the public opinion in the majority population and within their global network of contacts. This culminated in a dramatic confrontation in the renowned Alta affair, a case which became a turning-point in the relationship between the state and the Sami population in Norway, and a great step forward in the direction of a more extended, intense and public self-reflection within the Sami population.

The historical background of the Alta affair is that the Norwegian state planned, and later effectuated, the damming of the Alta-Kautokeino watercourse which flows through several central areas of Sapmi. The construction was seen as a threat to important grazing areas and calving places used by reindeer Sami, and as such would amount to an encroachment on the reindeer industry's natural resource base (Brantenberg 1985).

The construction plans prompted concern over the negative

46

ecological consequences to the salmon spawning areas, wild life and vegetation along the Alta river, and over the general destruction of a "pearl of natural beauty." The Sami Movement considered the construction an infringement of the Sami right to land and water in Sapmi. In light of these concerns, the Sami Movement, along with nature conservationists and large portions of the local population, mobilized to fight against the plans. This construction, which activated supporters and opponents for ten-twelve years and which culminated in a large scale act of civil disobedience and a resulting unprecedented police response, became an event of global dimensions. Hundreds of people, Sami and non-Sami, chained themselves together and lay down in front of the construction machines, were carried away by the police and subsequently fined. Participants from 10 different countries were noted during the Alta demonstrations (Lindal & Sunde 1981).

My aim here is not to present a representative picture of the Alta affair seen as an historical event through time, or as an ethno-drama (Bjørklund and Brantenberg 1981, Thuen 1983, Paine 1985). I shall attempt to illustrate how it sheds light on the positioning of the Sami in inter-cultural space and stress why it, in that sense, was an important event in the invention of Sami selfhood. The most fundamental message of the Sami Movement as it is inscribed in the Manifesto of 1979 (The Sami Political Programme, Charta 79 (1980)) is that the Sami possess a right, sanctioned by tradition and by virtue of their being a people, to nurture and develop their own culture, and that state powers are duty-bound to guarantee that these freedoms and rights be fulfilled. It points out that the Sami had institutionalized resource management in Sapmi before the Nordic peoples subjugated Sapmi, and through this had established a permanent right to the territory in their homeland. It claims that this, among other things, means that they have dominion over the natural resources in which Sami culture is anchored. During the 70s and 80s, the state granted certain concessions which seemed to indicate that it acknowledged its duties as far as the first component of this claim was concerned. This provided moral and financial support for a number of the projects about which the Sami Movement had issued demands and which comprised that sector called, in the language of bureaucrats, culture: the teaching of the Sami language, other Sami-oriented education, support for the Sami media, theatre, museums, etc. Demands referring to Sami dominion over land and water in Sapmi, on the other hand, were totally rejected as out of hand.

The Sami Movement's ethno-political participation in the Alta affair was founded upon the premise that tampering with the natural environment in Sapmi would entail the infringement of an old Sami enterprise and industry and would, therefore, constitute a violation of Sami culture. What was at stake was, namely, reindeer pastoralism – the enterprise which, in modern times, typified the distinctive Sami character, historical continuity, and traditional association with Sapmi. Reindeer herding, in a more factual sense, demonstrated the culture's bond with nature. The powerful symbolic significance of reindeer pastoralism contributed a great deal to the increase in support for the protest campaign which accrued from all segments of the Sami population. It was not only the Sami, however, who opposed the proposed dam construction. The affair generated attention and concern among Norwegians, populations in other Nordic countries and internationally as well. Nature conservationists in Norway and many other countries became important allies of the Sami Movement. Other important supporters were the organized indigenous peoples' movement, specially represented by the WCIP, other international organizations which work for indigenous and ethnic minorities rights, experts on international law, anthropologists, etc.

Until the 70s, the Sami waged a war of words in their fight to develop their culture on their own terms, and their message was generally ignored by the mass media. Under the threat of the damming of the Alta-Kautokeino watercourse, they began to make use of more spectacular means to arouse attention. The first Sami demonstrations with banners and slogans were organized and such demonstrations became more and more common both in various places in Sapmi and in Oslo as the anticipated start of construction drew near. In Oslo some Sami demonstrators pitched a *lávvu* [tipi-like tent originally used by the Sami when following herd migrations, which has now gained symbolic weight] in front of the Norwegian Parliament building *(Stortinget)* and demanded to speak to the Prime Minister. Others began a hunger strike. Some Sami women occupied the Prime Minister's office and demanded to have an audience with her. Sami delegations addressed themselves, time after time, to the government and to the leaders of the political parties. They also addressed their case in person to the Pope and to the UN. Others, chained together, sang patriotic songs, lay down in front of the construction machines and let themselves be carried away by the police (Paine 1985, Thuen 1983). This drama put the relationship between the Sami and the state powers in Norway in sharp relief.

The Alta affair generated formidable attention in and from the media. Film cuts from the event reached very nearly every home in Sapmi, the Nordic countries and as far away as Australia, North America and distant lands in South America. Sami spokesmen and -women presented through the media a picture of the Sami as an indigenous people with roots stretching back thousands of years, in a homeland, Sapmi, and as a people with global orientations which was in the process of acquiring a position as a modern, self-aware nation in inter-cultural space. But the division within the Sami population was also revealed. Disagreement over the use of civil disobedience and the radical demands concerning Sami self-determination in Sapmi split the Sami Movement into a radical wing and a moderate wing. The fulcrum of political gravity still lay in the Sami organizations which represented historical continuity in an ethno-political sense, but many considered the tactics used by the activists an improper rebellion against the authorities. In the end, the Sami lost the campaign against the dam construction, but the Alta affair proved to be a watershed in Sami ethno-political history.

Towards a new Sapmi: tendencies and perspectives

Clearly, the vision of Sami identity held by the pioneers of the Sami Movement gained support because of its reassessment and de-conventionalizing of the self-understanding that had been brought about by the asymmetrical majority/minority situation. Also it created the possibility for a shared Sami paradigm, placing the Sami in the context of a global movement which emphasized dignity and equality.

In spite of the slow pace with which the Sami Movement gained support during its first decade and the fact that there still are significant variations with regard to what individual Sami have appropriated and internalized of the vocabulary of knowledge for which the new self-understanding stands, the message was received favorably. Its appeal was that it provided a new foundation for thought, action and life orientation, and that it made possible a Sami fellowship which created a basis for self-confidence in inter-cultural matters. We have seen that the invention of this paradigm, and what can be understood as its operationalization, was accomplished by means of an exhaustive mediative procedure in which central aspects of Sami history, language, folklore and life style were transformed into signifiers of ethnic distinction and communality. These aspects became integrated in a vocabulary and a language of symbols which made it possible to speak of Sami distinctiveness and self-understanding internally, as well as externally in the inter-cultural space. In this mediation, nationalist rhetoric has occupied a central position, both explicitly and implicitly. This rhetoric has a structure which testifies to the fact that mediation is organized as an operation of double comparison. Firstly, it involves an objectification and glorification of a Sami estate – viewed **in relation to other peoples' estates.** Secondly, it concerns an objectification of a new and dignified life in which the Sami **themselves** can nurture and develop this estate. This new modality is constituted **in contrast to the past,** particularly that aspect of the past which betokens powerlessness and oppression and feelings of inferiority and ignorance (Ruong 1982).

In the process of communicating this newly-won self-understanding and self respect the Sami experienced a decrease in the traditional sense of powerlessness. They were in the process of gaining control over the creation of their own status as political players, dictating their terms of and production of knowledge and identity. The surrounding world gradually began to notice that the Sami presented an authoritative and vital knowledge of themselves in a language that resonated with inter-cultural standards of the production of knowledge and notions of a genuine, awakening nationalism. This then, lent authority and influence to the organizations and the elite within in the Sami population, who then were encouraged to further elaborate and internalize the paradigm and assume control over Sami self-presentation and ethno-political positioning.

The discourse on ethnic self-understanding and self-presentation has not become less intense in the Sami world since the Alta affair, but the interest in achieving, experiencing and affirming identity through confrontation with the outer world, particularly through confrontation with the *dáža,* which was of such importance in the first phase of the Sami Movement (Eidheim 1971), appears, in the period after the Alta affair, to have decreased significantly. The discourse is now more and more characterized by new questions and new issues and themes. The Sami now increasingly appropriate the life possibilities made available through education and prosperity. The possibilities inherent in the enormous expansion in the ways of organizing one's life also create ambivalence. The question of what it is to be a Sami, as more and more Sami attain positions and become exponents of life-styles which traditionally have been associated with the non-Sami world, becomes challenging and volatile.

The spokesmen and women of the Sami Movement, those in control of the definition, interpretation and representation of "Sami-ness" have not only acquired knowledge of Sami history and culture, attained proficiency in, and utilized, the Sami language, revising the language to accomodate the communication of modern phenomena, but they have also mastered foreign emblems of knowledge. In brief, they are found at the front lines in the creation of new intellectual and artistic expressions of what it means to be Sami. They produce new knowledge about the Sami language, history and culture. They formulate and drive home policies which advance the notion of the intrinsic value of Sami culture and which promote cultural progress. Also, they are directly and indirectly important links in the pan-Sami ethno-political network and they present, with success, the Sami in the inter-cultural and global space by means of their knowledge and ethno-political experiences, artistic achievements as well as cultural anchorage. It is this extended ethno-political orientation and activity, and the new diversity in life styles and occupations which represent Sami modernity.

Following the Alta affair, an increasing number of Sami have become familiar with and have assimilated the paradigm, based on Sami history, majority/minority dynamics, such notions as "we were here first," "we are a people," and "Sapmi is our cultural heritage," that was originally formulated by a tiny elite. This knowledge has not only been accepted as accurate and authentic, and has not only been collectivized, but it functions now more and more as conventionalized knowledge, as non-problematized and taken-for-granted categories of thought and action in the Sami world. Conventionalization of new knowledge naturally also implies de-conventionalization of old Sami wisdom. One reinvents Sami self-understanding of the past, so to speak, so that it may provide idiomatic material for comparison with what one wishes to accomplish in one's own time.

We may imagine that conventionalization takes place by means of negotiations which naturalize knowledge, which transform specific knowledge previously experienced and handled as new and germane, perhaps even controversial, into taken-for-granted knowledge by means of negotiations and, indeed, which reinterpret traditional knowledge. What, at any given time, are considered conventional, implicit or non-focused knowledge and orientations may be derived from interaction in concrete events and other discursive material. Since "Sami" clearly is a totalizing and precarious identity – such that nearly everything one does and thinks is a potential expression of one's Sami-ness, such negotiations will color the discourses of day to day life in Sami local societies. Discussions for and against the demands on the part of women for greater political influence, the intellectuals' ideas and life styles, anxiety about youth problems, commentaries about the neighbour's new house and their language habits and clothing preferences, their ways of bringing up their children - all these themes have inserted themselves into this negotiative aspect. This conventionalization aspect thus can be perceived as an unrecognized meta-aspect of daily life's concrete practices. Recognition and comprehension usually first appear in forms in which people discover that "something has changed" (Balto n.d., Stordahl 1994).

The discourse on lifestyle and ethnic authenticity (seen as signification work) absorbs the flow of an unordered multiplicity of semiotic material, but it also shows particular concern with particular issues and themes. Prominent are those which reflect an incremental readjustment of social differentiation in the Sami world: 1) The changing pattern of gender relations spurred on by an increasing number of educated and inter-culturally oriented women taking part in public life, in politics and in various branches of artistic activities to an increasing degree; 2) The changing relationship between generations throughout Sapmi, reflected in a general tendency among those born after WW II to make career decisions and to have world views and life styles that are significantly different than those of the previous generation. There are changes in family relations towards a pattern in which nuclear families operate more on their own independent of traditional networks of kin and ritual kin, and we have witnessed the development of a distinct youth culture; 3) The tendency towards a formation of a social hierarchy which involves the entire Sami world, for which education, pro-Sami ethno-political orientation and ideas, and cultural skills representing "Sami modernity" are high ranking criteria. An important aspect of this discourse may be seen as an attempt at clarifying the rules of relevance in the sifting of orientations and skills necessary in Sapmi today – a process which can, in addition, be decisive for social success/failure. This clarification, viewed as an aspect of the overall cultural development, does not keep pace with the new and confusing expressions and the many cultural inventions which pour in, and thus the volume and intensity of negotiations increase (Stordahl 1996). Sami social workers have suggested that the new age creates new forms of winners and losers, and have asserted that the increase in social problems – juvenile delinquency, failed marriages, broken homes, increased violence and suicides – must be seen in relation to this background. This implies that the constant negotiating of these new parameters not only generates integration of diversity and, in the long term, the conventionalization of knowledge, but they also create preconditions for cultural insecurity, personal frustration and the generation of new categories of social winners and losers.

The Sapmi of today is, in other words, a complex world, exhibiting social, cultural and political trends which, in some aspects, appear to be contradictory; a world in the process of transformation which, to many Sami individuals, appears bewildering and difficult to master. There are internal as well as external voices to be heard which claim that the Sami are rapidly losing their identity, while, on the other hand, others maintain that the Sami are an indigenous population which appears to be succeeding in establishing themselves as a distinct people in dialogue and interaction with the external, modern world.

I have seen it as my primary aim in this article to accentuate the main tendencies which have emerged during the course of a half century. I have wanted to show that if we are to look at the cultural dynamics in such a long-term perspective, it is possible to expose

certain developmental tendencies which together represent a continuous invention of a new, collective self-understanding. This
self-understanding is created by means of a process which is both
cognitive and political. It reorganizes and disseminates knowledge
of the Sami past and their cultural hallmark as a people, it reorganizes knowledge of the minority/majority relation, and, finally,
it reorganizes and incorporates knowledge, political/ideological
orientations and life style elements which circulate inter-culturally.
The long-term process shows that (and how) it is possible to adopt
and collectivize new and radically alien elements and, at the same
time, objectify and renew the experience of a fellowship which is
Sami.

Viewed from the perspective which has been briefly presented
here, we may conclude that the cultural representations which signal
the invention come about by adaptation and unification of internal
and external knowledge and thought (Eidheim 1993). The great
number of such representations are perhaps of such a simple and
domestic character that they are not immediately noticeable at all,
while others strike the eye at once. Some of them, of course, are
also considered controversial and are characterised by some as
"cultural cloning." That is to say, inventions in which various
traditional Sami idioms are provocatively combined with other,
alien idioms to make constructs with a "double signature." Several
such constructs have also been discovered by the outside world and
circulate inter-culturally as signs of contemporary Sami imagination,
life style, cultural creativity and national self-assertion. The most
conspicuous have to do with music, painting, sculpture and literature
(Lukkari 1987, 1991; Jåks 1981, 1988a, 1988b; Persen 1989;
Valkeapää 1988). A prominent example is the internationally renowned film *Ofelaš (Pathfinder)* directed by Nils Gaup (Gaup 1987).

The eighties and after

The political development of modern Sapmi has, in its essential features, been influenced by the Nordic context in which it exists. If we look at how the Sami Movement has organized its ethno-political project and what it has achieved, it is important to note that it has been able to play on and activate the fundamental cultural and political values to which these states make claim. As citizens of the liberal Nordic welfare states, the Sami have enjoyed the benefits of the welfare state along with the rest of the population. The Nordic countries, for their part, have, to a certain degree, been open to Sami demands for improved conditions in which to cultivate and develop culture, and have, by means of economic allocations and in other ways, supported reforms initiated by the Sami Movement. The Sami Movement has, in addition, found inspiration and strength in the international cooperation – especially the WCIP.

The Sami Movement's vision that the Sami be able to present themselves as a "unified, democratically organized people which is in a position to plan and conduct its own cultural development" still appears to be a promise of the future. The four involved states respond rather differently to the question of how far they will go in recognizing the Sami as an indigenous people and in giving their respective Sami populations extraordinary rights on an ethnic basis – combining the Sami's right to self-determination with the state's sovereignty is a delicate question both constitutionally and politically. Nevertheless, the Sami Movement views the establishment of transitional solutions to this dilemma, which may create a climate in which the question may gradually mature and be clarified, as an important step in the direction of greater self-determination. The reasons for this restrained optimism is that each of the Nordic states have legitimated and financed elective assemblies (Sami Parliaments) which should be able to discuss and coordinate Sami interests and be authoritative advocates for the Sami populace vis-à-vis the state. The Sami Parliament in Finland was established in 1975, in Norway in 1989, and lastly in Sweden in 1993.

The most radically reform-oriented core of the Sami Movement perceives Norway to be the country in which the Sami have attained the most, in terms of creating a platform from which to further develop Sami self-determination. In order to examine the reasons for this, it is necessary to return to the Alta affair and all its repercussions.

The Sami cause, dramatized and presented by the Sami Movement, and mediated by newspapers, radio and television, was politically decisive. The events created for many – for Sami as well as Norwegians – the surprising recognition that the Alta affair was not just about the construction of a dam in Norway, but that it also had to be seen as a Sami concern and an indigenous peoples' concern. The events created, in other words, new knowledge which legitimized the Sami Movement's demand that rights for the Sami as an indigenous population in Norway had to be reviewed, formulated and institutionalized.

The immediate consequence, in an ethno-political sense, was in fact that the Norwegian government appointed two important commissions, one with the mandate to investigate the Sami's total situation including the legal aspects (NOU 1984:18) and the other to investigate more specifically cultural and linguistic aspects (NOU 1985:14). Both were asked to propose reforms. This resulted, towards the end of the 80s, in the inclusion of a paragraph in the Norwegian constitution, informally referred to as the "Sami paragraph," which conferred upon the state the responsibility to guarantee that the Sami in Norway, by virtue of their being an indigenous people, would be able to preserve and develop their culture and society.

A "Sami law" was enacted which legalized the organization of an assembly, democratically elected by the Sami – the *Sámediggi*, (Nor. = *Sametinget)*. As part of this Sami law, a new language law was also approved which, in principle, equated Sami and Norwegian as official languages. And lastly, the Alta affair resulted in an increased endorsement of the self-assertionist line for which the Sami Movement had furnished the foundations. Many present day Sami now in their 30s and 40s, point out that the Alta affair represented a turning point in their self-understanding as Sami.

Although there existed, and still does, a divided opinion in the Sami population in Norway as to the argumentation and perspective on self-determination which had fostered these results, the establishment of the *Sámediggi* was officially celebrated in a mood of optimism and festivity. Olav V, the King of Norway, who was very popular and respected both by the Norwegian as well as the Sami population, was invited to the opening. The presence of the King not only added luster and gravity to the inauguration ceremony, but in his speech he also paid homage to the Sami as a distinct people possessing a vibrant culture, and emphasized the historical roots which bound the Sami to an expanse of land which now is divided between four nations. He made no secret of the fact that the Sami had not been considered equal to the majority population and expressed the wish that the Sami Parliament would prove to be a useful instrument for the Sami populace in coordinating and in advancing their interests, and creating a more egalitarian relationship with the majority population. This inauguration, and the events which lead up to it, have been characterised as the start of a new epoch in the history of the Sami.

The "Sami paragraph" in the Norwegian Constitution, the founding of the Sami Parliament and the new language law aroused attention and interest far beyond the Nordic countries. It was considered to be, in the case of indigenous people, a pioneering step which also attracted attention in international forums.

The Sami Parliament in Norway began functioning in 1989. It has mainly functioned as an advisory body for the state since the extent of its formal authority and the areas over which it has jurisdiction are matters still awaiting clarification, and the recognition of the Sami's territorial rights to "land and water" have not been determined. These questions are the subject of intense debates both among Sami and Norwegians. Many things indicate, however, that the Sami Parliament, has already attained a significant level of de facto authority. This is evident in the attention paid by the majority population, especially in Northern Norway, to the Sami Parliament. Regional administrative bodies such as municipalities and county councils, confederacies of occupational organizations and other organizations have taken the Sami Parliament seriously. Sami political representatives are now participants in a number of cooperative projects at the national level, and we also find them participating as members in a number of inter-state organizations – the Commission for the Barent's Region, CSCE and others.

The Sami Movement hopes that the official recognition won by the Sami population in Norway and the position and authority granted the Sami Parliament will form a model for a similar development of the relationship between the state and the Sami populations in Finland, Russia and Sweden. The Movement is working to persuade the three countries that the establishment of a common body through which the Sami of all the Nordic countries could better coordinate their activities would be both useful and a natural extension of the development up to now. It is also working to assist the Sami population in Russia in establishing a viable ethno-political organization which would thus provide for Sami representation in all of the four nations. It is in this way that the Sami Movement is aspiring to continue its work by extending and strengthening an organizational and cultural fellowship, and, thereby, strengthening the Sami hope for survival as a small, distinct people in Europe's northernmost part.

1   This article is adapted from several earlier works by the same author, notably
    Eidheim 1971 and 1992 (cf. references).

References:

Aikio, S. 1980. *Sámiid historjá,* Kautokeino, Sami Instituhtta.

Balto, A. (MS n.d.). *Barn, kultur og samfunn.*

Barth, F. 1969. *Ethnic Groups and Boundaries,* Oslo, Universitetsforlaget.

Barth, F. 1994. *Manifestasjon og prosess*, Oslo, Universitetsforlaget.

Birketvedt, B. F. 1991. "Hvem har signert?" Et antropologisk perspektiv på kunst
i Nord-Norge, *Ottar* nr. 5/91.

Bjørklund, I. og Brantenberg, T. 1981. *Samisk reindrift - norske inngrep,* Oslo,
Universitetsforlaget.

Boine, Mari. 1989. *Gula, gula.* (LP Album) Idut, Iggaldas, 9710 Indre Billefjord,
Norway.

Brantenberg, O. T. 1985. "The Alta-Kautokeino Conflict, Sami Reindeer Herding
and Ethno-Politics," in Brøsted, et al, *Native Power,* Oslo, Universitetsforlaget.

Dyck, N. (ed.) 1985. *Indigenous Peoples and the Nation State. Forth World
Politics in Canada, Australia and Norway,* Institute of Social and Economic
Research, St. John's, Newfoundland.

Dædnugádde nuorat 1974. (LP Album) MAI 7402, Oslo.

Eidheim, H. 1985. "Indigenous Peoples and the State: The Saami Case in
Norway," in J. Brønsted et al (eds.), *Native Power. The Quest for Autonomy
and Nationhood of Indigenous Peoples,* Oslo, Universitetsforlaget.

Eidheim, H. 1971. *Aspects of the Lappish Minority Situation,* Oslo, Universitetsforlaget, Also published in Oslo Occasional Papers in Social Anthropology
No. 14, 1990. Department and Museum of Anthropology, University of Oslo.

Eidheim, H. 1992. *Stages in the Development of Sami Selfhood,* Working Paper
No. 7, Department and Museum of Anthropology, University of Oslo.

Eidheim, H. 1993. "Bricolage and ingeniørverksemd i Sámpi," *Norsk Sosialantro-
pologi 1993 - et utsnitt.* Norges Forskningsråd (ed.), Oslo.

Fokstad, P. 1966. "Litt om det samiske problem sett innenfra," *Sameliv* 1964-66,
Oslo.

Fossbakk, B. 1987. "Doudji. Samisk tradisjon i en moderne tid," *Ottar* nr. 2/87.

Gaski, H. 1988. "Den nye joiken. Om mottakelsen av Ailo Gaups første diktsam-
ling," *Edda* vol. 1.

Gaup, A. 1982. *Joiken og kniven,* Oslo, Gyldendal Norsk Forlag.

Gaup, N. *Ofelaš [Pathfinder]*, Film produced by John M. Jacobsen, Filmkameratene AS, Oslo.

Henriksen, A.J. og Johnskareng, A. 1976. *Guovssahas* (LP Album) Jår'galead'dji, Tana.

Johnsen, K. 1972. "Hva er det som får en same til å bli sameaktivist," *Aftenposten* 16th May.

Jernsletten, R. 1986. *Samebevegelsen i Norge. Idé og strategi 1900-1940,* Unpublished Cand. Philol. thesis, University of Tromsø.

Jåks, I. 1988a. *Vår tids støtter* [The Pillars of our time], Sculpture, Karasjok.

Jåks, I. 1988b. *Stille vender tanken,* [Calmly the thought turns], Sculpture.

Lindal, Å. og Sunde, H. 1981. *Alta-bilder, Alta pictures.* (Text in Norwegian and English), Oslo, Pax forlag AS.

Lukkari, R. M. 1987. *Mørk dagbok,* (Translated from Sami by Laila Stien and Harald Gaski), Karasjok, Davvi Media.

Lukkari, R. M. 1991. *Min konges gylne klær,* (Trans. from Sami by Laila Stien), Oslo, Gyldendal Norsk Forlag.

Mathisen, H. R. 1975. *Sápmi.* Tromsø.

NOU 1984:18. *Om samenes rettsstilling,* Justisdepartementet, Oslo.

NOU 1985:14. *Samisk kultur og utdanning,* Kultur- og vitenskapsdepartementet, Oslo.

Paine, R. 1984. "Norwegians and Saami: Nation-State and Fourth World," in G.L. Gold (ed.), *Minorities and Mother Country Imagery,* Institute of Social and Economic Studies. St. John's, Newfoundland.

Paine, R. 1985. "Ethno-Drama and the Fourth World. The Sami Action Group in Norway 1979-1981," in Dyck, N. (ed.), *Indigenous Peoples and the Nation State. Fourth World Politics in Canada, Australia and Norway,* Social and Economic Papers 14, Memorial University of Newfoundland, St. Johns.

Rajala, B. 1990. "To kvinnelige samiske lyrikere. Om Kirsti Paltto og Rauni Magga Lukkari," *Ottar* 2/90 .

Roung, I. (MS n.d.). *Om en helhetssyn på samernas verklighet,* Sámi Instituhtta archive, Kautokeino.

Stordahl, V. 1996. *Same i den moderne verden,* Karasjok, Davvi Girji o.s.

Thuen, T. 1983. *Meaning and Transaction in Sami Ethno-politics,* MS, Department of Anthropology/Sami Studies, University of Tromsø, Tromsø.

Utsi, E. 1976. "Sameland i våre hjerter," *Nordkalotten* 11/33 .

Valkepää, N. A. 1990. *Solen min far,* (Translated from Sami by Harald Gaski, Jon Todal and Kristina Utsi-Boine), DAT, Kautokeino.

Einar Niemi

Sami History and the Frontier Myth

*A Perspective on Northern Sami Spatial
and Rights History*

The Nordic frontier

In the opening passages of his famous novel *Markens grøde*
(Growth of the Soil, 1917), Knut Hamsun describes his hero Isak
Sellanraa's long wandering into "wilderness – across the marshes
and into the forests" in search of a suitable place to clear ground for
his backwoods farm. It is an evocative story of a pioneer who was
the first to find his way to the virgin northern mountain valleys
which were waiting for the peasant's plough and scythe. Hamsun's
picture of the pioneer is a heroic one, of the lonely giant who fought
the wilderness. His "great commons owned by nobody, the land
without landlords" was a no man's land, with connotations of the
classic territorial-juridical doctrines of *terra nullius* and *terra
incognita* (Niemi 1994 I).

Hamsun's notion of the open, free territory is parallel to the
American frontier theory elaborated by the historian Fredrick
Jackson Turner towards the end of the nineteenth century in his
attempts at explaining the development of certain characteristic
features of American society. The frontier stood for a moving,
flexible border between the areas inhabited by the white settlers
moving westward and the unconquered territories beyond.

This notion of the frontier has been adopted by the Norwegian
social scientist Ottar Brox in his description of the spatial and economic expansion in North Norway in the period 1800-1950. He
labels North Norway "the frontier of the Nordic countries," offering

new possibilities for territorial and economic expansion. Those who exploited the frontier options were primarily fishermen and peasants moving in from the south. One central thesis is that the traditional economy of the north was extremely tenacious. Even in the first decades after World War II, it was principally characterized as a subsistence economy. A core prerequisite for this was the open, rich natural resources and the frontier situation (Brox 1984).

Even if central aspects of Brox' descriptions and analysis have been argued against (Drivenes 1985 I, 1985 II; Fulsås 1986), his version of the frontier theory applied to North Norway has been influential, with implications also for interpretations of Sami history. Moreover, attitudes and opinions presupposing such a theory have historical roots, although the strength and vigour by which they have been advocated have varied over time, depending on the ideology of the age as well as on real political forces, both with clear Sami historical implications.

Border territories and state rivalries

Historically large tracts of the northern regions of Norway, Sweden, Finland and Russia were called Finnmark (or plural: Finnmarkene), or alternatively, Lapland, or, in Sami, Sapmi. The term Lapland had become, until recently, the internationally accepted designation, originally meaning, as the etymology of the term indicates, "the land of the Sami," as does the name Finnmark (in reference to the old Norwegian ethnonym for the Sami). The old Finnmarkene stretched far to the south; into Norway as far south as Røros and into Sweden to the Jämtland mountains. As an academic debate and as a political reality, however, the southern border of the Sami spatiality has been a highly disputed issue for about a century (Haarstad 1981, 1992; Bergsland 1994).

Since the Middle Ages the northern Sami habitation area was regarded as a border territory between cultures and ethnic groups and between east and west. Until the High Middle Ages the northern border of the Norwegian settlement of fishermen and peasants along the coast was at the Malangen fjord – where the city of Tromsø is located (founded in 1794). The territories north and east of Malangen were regarded by the southern states as *terra nullius*, the border zone to Finnmark, inhabited solely by Sami, both on the coast and inland. Norwegian seasonal hunters and traders and tax collectors exploited Finnmark. The coast of Finnmark was also important for trader-chieftains from Hålogaland, the old designation of Northern Norway south of Malangen, as a sea route to a famous market place at the mouth of the Dvina river on the southern shores of the White Sea. During the Viking Age the Norwegian king claimed both trade and taxation rights over the Sami, breaking down the power of the Northern Norwegian chieftains.

Finnmark was the last large region to be integrated into the Norwegian state, and, as was often the case, political expansion was linked to religion. In the thirteenth century a church established at Tromsø served as the northernmost religious center for missionaries working among the Sami. In a papal letter concerning this missionary outpost in the service of the Roman Catholic Church it is stated that the Tromsø church was situated *"juxta pagones"* – near the pagans.

At the end of the thirteenth or in the early fourteenth century, state and church expansion into Finnmark and the extension of the littoral Norwegian fishing and peasant settlements began in earnest. The main economic mechanism behind this was the new, favorable European market for northern Norwegian stockfish, with the Hanseatic League as market intermediaries (Nielssen 1994). Thus the classic, instrumental state-building alliance was established: church building, state body establishment, and settlement. As early as 1307 the church of Vardø was consecrated, in the utmost peripheral border area towards Russia. Soon after a royal fortress, Vardøhus, was built at the same place, as a marker of Norwegian state political ambitions. Finnmark was formally turned into a royal fief, with the

Vardøhus fortress as seat. A string of Norwegian fishing stations and villages were established along the coast east to the Varanger fjord, with Vardø the largest, becoming an urban center.

In spite of the fact that there were not yet any formally agreed upon state borders, the Danish-Norwegian kingdom declared its sovereignty in the coastal regions of Finnmark, declaring the Arctic Ocean *mare nostrum* – "our sea" or "the King's sea." The inland areas, however, were as early as 1326, by way of a treaty defined as joint territories *(Fellesdistrikter)* between Sweden, Denmark-Norway and Novgorod, in which the collaborating states had equal rights to taxation and trade. Despite the fact that the Danish-Norwegian state's political and economic integration endeavours were primarily confined to the coastal regions, the Sami were, nonetheless influenced through taxation, trade and missionary advances.

Throughout the Late Middle Ages the other northern states also launched state building activities in the borderless inland, through church building, peasant colonization, establishment of local state administrative bodies, and partly by military enterprises. The main background for the state rivalry was this area's economic and strategic importance, also linked to the sixteenth century dream of the North East Passage, awakened by modern geography and the "Great Discoveries." A northern commercial sea route to the Far East would mean a dramatically increased economic and strategic importance for Finnmark, both as a market center and transit port. Non-Nordic European sea-faring nations, such as England and the Netherlands, were also engaged in the competition for natural resources, and trade and sea routes in the far north. The escalation of the international tension threatened to develop into war involving England at the end of the 16th century. Wars which were actually fought on the "the Finnmark question" were, however, restricted to the northern powers, first between Russia and Sweden, then the Kalmar War (1611-13) between Denmark-Norway and Sweden.

After Denmark-Norway's victory in the Kalmar War Sweden

withdrew its claims to the northern coastal areas, which meant that the littoral Sami in the area between Tysfjord in Northern Nordland and the Varanger fjord in Eastern Finnmark became Norwegian subjects. The state's integration endeavours in the north were propelled through mercantilist trade policies and administrative reforms, i.e. the implementation of a regional bureaucracy. Finnmark was officially designated a county, and, as such, hosted a govenor's seat on a year-round basis.

In the 18th century, particularly after the Great Nordic War (1701-1720), it became evident to the Nordic states that formal borders were necessary in the north, and the border treaties of 1751 and 1826 were agreed on as a result of diplomacy and collaboration. In both treaties limited provisions were made to protect Sami traditional rights. In a codicil to the 1751 treaty traditional Sami seasonal trans-border migrations, including reindeer herding, fishing and hunting were mentioned. In the 1826 treaty the old Eastern Sami seasonal movements between inland districts and the Arctic coast in South Varanger were guaranteed as an interim provision.

State borders were not established in the northernmost parts of Fennoscandia until the end of the eighteenth and the early nineteenth century; between Sweden and Norway in 1751 and Russia and Norway in 1826. This vast area has after WW II been named the North Calotte, covering the northernmost counties of Norway (Nordland, Troms and Finnmark), Sweden (Norrbotten) and Finland (Lapland). As a result of increased contact and cooperation with Russia in later years, the Murmansk region has also been defined as a part of the North Calotte. The North Calotte concept has now, to some degree been superseded by the Barents Euro-Arctic Region (Stokke & Tunander 1994; Dellenbrant & Olsson 1994) – a transnational, regional cooperative political body made up of Norway, Sweden, Finland and Russia, established in 1992.

In the long run the state borders meant real cleavages in the Sami territories and increased pressures on traditional territorial rights. This reflected real historical development, including settlement of new groups of people, industrial enterprises and governmental security policy considerations, as well as growing anti Sami juridical attitudes. Probably no other Sami group experienced so heavily this development as the Eastern Sami (the Skolt Sami) in the border regions of Norway, Finland and Russia. The Neiden East Sami group were eventually driven from their winter territories in Finland and settled permanently in their spring and summer camp in Neiden in South Varanger. The Pasvik East Sami were Russian subjects, who, during the inter-war period became Finnish subjects as a result of the Finnish conquest of "the Arctic Corridor." In the 1920s "the Pasvik East Sami problem" was "solved" through an arrangement between the Norwegian and Finnish governments in which the rights were "bought out" by the two governments. The Sami were paid a sum of money to end their traditional treks across the border (Eriksen & Niemi 1981; Andresen 1989; Vorren 1989, Niemi 1994 II; Wikan 1995).

Sami indigenous rights

In the sixteenth century the fisheries deteriorated, partly because of less favorable markets and partly due to the depletion of salt water fish resources in North Norway. Many Norwegians moved from the outer coast areas into the fjords which hitherto had been almost completely inhabited by Sami and which were well suited to a combined economy of fishing and cattle breeding (Niemi 1983; Nielssen 1986; Odner 1992). In the Late Middle Ages another ethnic group, the *Kvens,* originally coming from the area around the Gulf of Bothnia, began to settle in Finnmark. The ethnonym Kven was, and still is, the Norwegian name for the Finnish settlers in Northern Norway and their descendants. In the early eighteenth century a regular migration of Kvens took place, from the Finnish and Swedish parts of Lapland and the Gulf of Bothnia coast to the river valleys and fjord heads in Finnmark and the northern parts of the county of

Troms. In general this was a peasant migration, a result of population pressures in the more populated farming areas to the south. In the nineteenth century the volume of Kvens in Troms and Finnmark increased dramatically. Now the influx took more the shape of modern labor migrations, with the fast expanding fishing stations and coastal towns as the main destinations (Niemi 1977, 1992 I, 1995 I; Jokipii 1982).

In this way the Sami in Finnmark were squeezed between two encroaching immigrant streams: Norwegian settlers from the outer coast, and Kvens from the inland. In addition to the physical displacement implicit in this double sided pressure, a cultural collision also took place. Although specialized reindeer herding had developed since the 1600s, the Sami way of life was still highly differentiated and most Sami, both those living in the inland and in the fjords, exploited a variety of resources through the different seasons of the year, involving seasonal migrations and extensive husbandry. This stood in contrast to the Kvens' intensive tillage of the ground and permanent farm settlements. The Kvens, however, were regarded by the authorities as agricultural innovators in the north due to their farming techniques and their settlement organization. They were thus eagerly welcomed as the Danish-Norwegian King's subjects. In this sense their presence in the thinly populated border regions signalled state sovereignty.

From the end of the eighteenth century immigration of peasants from well-established agricultural communities in the southern parts of Norway began to contribute to agricultural innovation in the north. The peasant colonization by these *døler* [valley people] of fertile valleys many places in Northern Norway, even on the very border to Russia in Eastern Finnmark, viz. the Pasvik and Grense Jakobselv valleys, was partly a product of a state expansionist policy that aimed at strengthening the permanent settlements with an influx of industrious settlers who would contribute to the economy of the region (Niemi 1994), and partly a result of push and pull mechanisms related to natural resources and demographic factors.

Although the influx of new settlers in the Sami areas clearly increased competition for land and water resources, resulting in episodic clashes and conflicts, the Sami were not immediately put on the defensive. The maintenance of Sami traditional rights was in some districts demonstrated by the fact that newcomers into many of the Sami areas were assimilated – they were allotted land and fishing rights, and intermarried on Sami terms. The integration of Norwegians and, in particular, Kvens into the Sami local societies more often than not involved the adoption of Sami language and clothing. The assimilation was not one sided, however, but was rather a synthesis, and today often remnants of the Kvens' original ethnicity and culture can be seen in family names and building traditions.

To some extent Sami traditional rights were respected by the authorities as well as by Norwegian and Kven immigrants. This is seen, for example, in numerous court decisions in favor of the Sami claims to land rights and title (Tønnesen 1978; Bratrein 1984; Bjørklund 1985; Hansen 1986; Eriksen 1993; Niemi 1994 II; Pedersen 1994). There are several reasons why the authorities respected Sami claims to traditional rights. Firstly, the Danish-Norwegian dynastic state was in reality a multicultural state with relaxed attitudes towards ethnic groups and minorities. In the north the state representatives often referred to the Sami as an "indigenous nation" with "aboriginal rights," in such phrases as "the oldest people of the land," "the first nation," etc. In the wake of the Napoleonic Wars, after approximately 1815, Romantic ideas strengthened this "first nation" doctrine related to the Sami. Historical-juridical studies in later years have documented that Sami traditional rights, in particular land title rights, were, prior to the 1800s, largely practiced and respected in Sami areas under Danish-Norwegian rule, and also in areas under the Swedish crown (Korpijaako 1994). Secondly, in the state's policy towards development in the north, often referred to as "whole-state policy" *(helstatspolitikk)*, especially under the influence of late mercantilist and physiocratic ideas, the state regarded the Sami way of life as highly important because of its exclusive demands on resource niches for which there were no competitors, i.e. the mountain reindeer pastures. The Sami were of economic importance both for trade and taxation. In addition all experience told that none of the other groups managed periods of economic depression as well as the Sami, due to their position, balanced between market and subsistence economy (Hansen 1984, 1990).

Lastly, because of the unclear border situation, the state preferred, during this period, to earn the loyalty of the Sami rather than to alienate them. Treaties settling issues of territorial sovereignty tended to result in lenient Norwegian attitudes towards Sami traditional rights. This is seen in the aftermath of the Kalmar War and after the border treaties of 1751 and 1826, when the littoral Sami living between the fjords of Tysfjord in the south and Varanger in the northeast became Norwegian subjects. After the borders were formally agreed upon, the states' rivalries over the Sami in the borderland, in which the states vied for Sami allegiance by offering more favorable treatment, came to an end. This rivalry for Sami loyalties also applied to Russia whose main instrument of territorial expansion, the Orthodox Church, was well experienced in missionary work in multi-cultural surroundings, and treated the Sami with greater respect than the western countries did (Niemi 1994 I).

Nation building and assimilation policy

Towards the end of the eighteenth century new attitudes towards the Sami traditional rights and minority rights in general began to appear, although a definitive shift did not come until the middle of the next century. Notions such as "equal rights in the local society" gradually replaced the ideas of exclusive, traditional rights for the indigenous group (Tønnesen 1972/79).

A local court case in 1848 in the village of Neiden in South Varanger, close to the Norwegian-Russian border, in which the Eastern Sami, the original population of the village, fought newly arrived Kven settlers marked the definitive end of the pro-Sami juridical regime. The issue was about the right to the rich salmon fishing in the Neiden River, traditionally considered to belong to the Neiden Sami. The court however, ruled that salmon fishing should from, that point on, be an equal right for everybody living in the village, irrespective of ethnic background or time of settlement (Tønnesen 1972/79; Niemi 1994 II; Wikan 1995). The implication of this court decision was that the Neiden Sami inevitably were put on the defensive because they now constituted a minority group in the village. The Kven influx had created a Kven dominant majority far more numerous than the members of the few old Sami family units.

At the same time, "the doctrine of the unregistered ground in Finnmark" was developed by Norwegian authorities. This doctrine, which has been the juridical basis for all the laws and regulations which have been passed on land territories in Finnmark from the middle of the nineteenth century until the present, claimed that the state had full ownership of all ground in the county not formally in private possession (Sandvik 1980, 1993 I). It was not until the academic and political debate brought on by the Alta-affair that this doctrine was challenged (Sandvik 1980; Minde 1991, 1993 I), especially after Sverre Tønnesen's ground-breaking study *Jorden i Finnmark* [The Ground of Finnmark] (Tønnesen 1972/79). Without a doubt "the doctrine of the unregistered ground in Finnmark" paved the way for a revival of frontier ideas related to the northern territories.

The new policies towards land and water rights in the mid 1800s were part of a more general minority policy which addressed both of the minority ethnic groups in the north – the Sami and the Kvens. This new policy was aimed at assimilating the two groups into the larger society. While the Sami and the Kvens previously had been regarded as important state subjects in the north, they now were defined as "foreign nations," a phrase inflated in the rhetoric of public reports throughout the second half of the nineteenth century. The general background for this new minority policy was Norwegian nationalism and nation building – a particular manifestation of Nationalist movements and ideologies throughout Europe at this time.

The more specific explanation of the assimilation policy was to be found in the cultural and geo-political situation in the north: the Sami and Kvens shared a border with Russia and were seen as a security threat to the Norwegian authorities. Russia was in western European political and diplomatic spheres increasingly depicted as a menace, and distrust and antagonism between Norway and Russia escalated, even though recent historical research has shown that such a menace in reality never existed. Sweden and Norway's policy of neutrality and appeasement towards Russia officially ended with the November Treaty (1855) which was signed by the allied Western powers as a political and diplomatic instrument against Russia. The existence of the Pomor Trade, the barter trade between Russian seafarers and people in Northern Norway, also caused much political anxiety and added to notions of a Russian threat.

An influx of Finns into Northern Norway did little to appease politicians' fears. In contrast to the sporadic and light migrations of former periods, the nineteenth century migration was massive and resulted in a high number of Kven settlements in the fjords and on the coast. By the time of the census of 1891 the Kvens amounted to 23 percent of the total population of Finnmark, with the Sami and the Norwegians at 32 and 45 percent respectively. The Kvens often settled in segregated "Kven towns" and "Kven villages," providing favorable conditions for the maintenance of Finnish as the primary language and other specific cultural and ethnic features. In addition, after 1809, Sweden lost Finland to Russia. Although the Grand Duchy of Finland retained considerable autonomy, it, and by extension the Kvens, were viewed with suspicion by the West and seen as a potential "fifth column," as disguised Russian infiltrators into Western Europe. Finally, the rise of Finnish Nationalism from the

1860s, in Sweden and Norway often referred to as "Fennomania," contributed to the suspicions and, in a way, collided with Norwegian (and Swedish) nationalist movements.[1]

Like the Kvens, the Sami were also seen as a security problem. In general they lived in the northern areas defined as "the vulnerable border districts," being neighbors and even relatives to Kvens. By the middle of the nineteenth century, the Sami constituted roughly one-half of the population of Finnmark, and yet they are reported to have been only minimally integrated into Norwegian society, with the knowledge of Norwegian not widespread. Seen from the point of view of Norwegian security interests and in terms of a general expansionist policy, ethnic and cultural pluralism was intolerable, as was the fact that Sami and Kvens in the border areas often lived geographically isolated from the Norwegian local communities.

The Norwegian policy of assimilation did not differentiate between Sami and Kvens, but adopted the holistic *fornorskningspolitikk* [the policy of Norwegianization]. In a similar manner, districts which were considered to be in the process of adopting the Norwegian language and culture were designated *overgangsdistrikter* [transition districts]. The policy began with cultural education, directed at schools and the church. The main battle was over language and identity, the main battlefield was the classroom, and the rank and file soldiers were the school teachers. In later phases, i.e. from the turn of the century until World War II, the cultural policy measures were escalated and further refined. In addition new fields and means were adopted to implement the policy, as economic enterprises, to a certain extent involving *Berufsverbot* [occupational inhibition] for members of the minority groups, and military build-up, including surveillance of the Sami and Kven settlements (Eriksen & Niemi 1981; Jernsletten 1986 II; Eriksen 1991; Niemi 1992 I, 1995; Drivenes 1992; Sandvik 1993 II).

Sami ethnopolitical mobilization

Throughout the period of Norwegianization, however, there were always some voices, mostly scholars, that were in favor of a separate, more tolerant policy towards the Sami based on their rights as an indigenous people. After the turn of the century the clergy and Sami ethnopolitical leaders also voiced their protests. The first period of modern Sami ethnopolitical organization, from the early years of the twentieth century until the 1920s, saw considerable political success. During this period, for example, Isak Saba, a Sami school teacher was elected M.P. to Stortinget [the Norwegian Parliament] for two terms on a Sami political program adopted by the Labor Party. Sami organizational work never, however, managed to change or moderate the Norwegianization policy during this period (Minde 1980, 1994, 1995; Jernsletten 1986 I; Drivenes & Jernsletten 1994). The forces mobilized in favor of the Norwegianization policy were too strong. In addition to *Realpolitik* related to the northern border security questions, the ideologies of nationalism and nation-building merged with other current ideological trends well suited to a discriminatory and repressive minority policy, informed by notions of Social Darwinism and even racism.

Suggestions that individual policies ought to be instituted towards the Kvens and the Sami as separate ethnic minorities were raised, both by scholars, Sami organizations and a few politicians. Their main argument was that the Kvens were immigrants who had voluntarily come to Norway and thus should be assimilated as rapidly as possible. The Sami, in contrast, were an indigenous people in Finnmark. While there always were voices in favor of a pro-Sami policy, there were hardly any who spoke for a more lenient policy towards the Kvens.

The Norwegian authorities defined the minority policy holistically as they neither had the resources nor sufficient knowledge to differentiate between the Sami and the Kvens. In addition, this policy which treated each group as a generic "minority" was justi-fied from an ideological and security standpoint.

Sami rights, European civilization and the frontier myth revisited

From the middle of the nineteenth century until World War II, Norwegianization was the official Norwegian minority policy. Though there were voices in favor of a more pluralistic policy towards the Sami, such an option succumbed to the pressures of nationalism, nation building, security policy, and modernization.

An integral part of this dominant ideology was the notion that the northern parts of Norway were the last stronghold of European civilization in the North against "Eastern barbarism." Here the "civilized house of Europe" bordered "Asian anarchy and chaos." In the rhetorics of the time there are abundant references to the idea of a specific historic mission: "Civilization" against "barbarism"; "culture" versus "chaos"; "law" versus "anarchy"; "progress" ver-sus "backwardness"; "Germanic race" versus "Mongolian race," etc. Institutions built by the Norwegian government in the north, such as schools and churches, were, in fact, often referred to as "cultural fortresses" against the East. The outcome was a Nordic version of the "White Man's Burden" with regards to the policy towards the Sami (Niemi 1995 II).

In the second half of the nineteenth and the earliest decades of the twentieth century North Norway experienced unprecedented economic and demographic expansion. The fisheries experienced strong growth, both due to favorable market conditions and abundant resources. Modern industry was introduced in the areas of mining, fish processing and whaling. The towns and fishing villages went through modern urbanization processes. Also new territorial expansion took place, nurturing the old doctrine of terra nullius and undermining remnants of Sami indigenous rights.

The "frontier" now moved in different directions. The inland valleys were more intensely exploited by the *døler* [peasant farmers]. The mountain regions saw the opening of modern mines which were often backed by international capital and foreign investments. Norwegian immigrants also moved across the Norwegian-Russian border and settled on the Murman Coast of the Kola Peninsula – originally a Sami area. These immigrants were to help in the development of this half-forgotten corner of the Russian Empire, and were thus initially welcomed by the tsarist regime (Sæther 1992; Nielsen 1991, 1992). The real "new" frontier, however, was the Arctic Ocean, now opened up by Northern Norwegian hunters and fishermen, especially the sealers who found new hunting grounds both in the western and the eastern waters of the Arctic. As a result of this, questions of sovereignty arose over the Arctic islands, from Greenland in the west to Novaja Zemlja in the east. From the turn of the century until the inter-war period the Norwegian Arctic policy took a rather aggressive turn, referred to by some historians as "the imperialism of the Arctic Ocean" (Berg 1994).

The minority policy of the North, the neglect of Sami rights and the frontier policy of the Arctic Ocean can be viewed as parts of one grand idea – the integrated and expanded Norwegian nation in the north. In the inter-war period the Sami were an ethnic minority experiencing a lack of social status as well as political influence. In the wider political context and compared to the earlier phases of the assimilationist policy, they also saw reduced interest for their fate in state political circles. They were marginalized on the political agenda as well as in society.

Sami political dilemmas

After World War II, the minority policies towards the Kvens and the Sami have developed in opposite directions. The Kvens have largely been defined as being without a special minority status in a political

76

sense, in spite of a nation-wide Kven political organization and growing self-awareness (Niemi 1995 IV). The Sami, on the other hand, have both been instrumental in and the beneficiaries of a new governmental policy that is based on the principles of cultural pluralism and indigenous rights articulated by international organizations, such as the ILO and the UN, culminating in the implementation of a fundamentally new, pro-Sami policy in the 1980s (Brantenberg 1991; Thuen 1995).

While the rights of the Sami to maintain their culture and language and to establish representative political bodies of their own have been guaranteed by law (the Sami Language Act, known as "the Sami Law" in the Sami Parliament/*Sámediggi*), and by an amendment to the constitution, the old questions of land and water rights remain unresolved. A central part of the Sami Rights Committee's mandate (given by the Norwegian government in 1980) is to study historically the issue of Sami rights and to contribute to the implementation of Norway's minority policy – namely to secure for the Sami their own culture, economy and society (Eidheim 1985; Brantenberg 1985, 1991; Thuen 1995). The Sami Rights Committee has, since its first report to the government in 1984 (NOU 1984:18), worked with the question of territorial rights in Finnmark. In 1993 and 1994 two preliminary reports on the issue were published (NOU 1993:34, NOU 1994:21) both resulting in heated public debates in which the Committee's attitudes were debated as well as the historical and contemporary realities related to land use. The final, concluding report on land and water rights and management in the county of Finnmark was published early in 1997.

The report (NOU 1997:4) states a principle that land rights should not be given on "indivual ethnic basis," but rather shared by the local population within defined geographical areas, irrespective of ethnic roots. Further, different models of natural resource management are represented by Sami and Norwegians elected by the Sami Parliament and the Finnmark County Parliament which have equal representation. At the same time, the Sami Rights Committee

77

published an expert report on civil and indigenous rights discussed in national and international contexts (NOU 1997:5). Formally the report is regarded as basis for the Sami Rights Committee. However, its considerations to some extent are a severe critique of the Sami Rights Committee's principles and many of its motions.

In the current debate it is possible to distinguish frontlines in opinion, both linked to history and to today's still existing ethnic, economic and geo-political conflicts in Finnmark. These are the frontlines of opinion between coast and inland Sami; between urbanized centers and the countryside; between Sami, Norwegians and Kvens, with shifting alliances; and between reindeer herding Sami on the one hand and peasants and farmers, independent of ethnic roots, on the other hand. The basic issues are, firstly, the question of documented historical rights, secondly, the question of current and future rights based on ethnicity, alternatively on geographic criteria, and, thirdly, the practical management of land and territorial rights, including administrative models. Should there be a separate Sami administrative body (the Sami Parliament or another Sami institution established for this specific task)? Another alternative is that the existing state and regional political bodies, operating on county level, are mandated to the task. And a third model is a combined management, in which both Sami and Norwegian state and county bodies have equal responsibility, Sami and Norwegian representatives working together in a joint body.

In the debate following the Sami Rights Committee's preliminary reports as well as the concluding report on Finnmark, some Sami politicians as well as scholars have accused the committee of defocusing historical Sami rights and of a biased presentation of the state's land rights. Further, the committee has been criticized for not analyzing the Sami land tenure issues in the context of international indigenous peoples' rights, for example in comparison to issues in North America and Australia. Both the committee and the state authorities have been described as conservative and reactionary in their attitudes, lagging behind the international developments in indigenous land rights (Brantenberg 1995; Minde 1995; Jull 1995).

Obviously, the Sami Rights Committee has faced a difficult task in its final deliberations, as have the Norwegian authorities. This is partly due to inherited inter-ethnic tensions and inborn prejudices, but it is also due to the history of the spatial patterns and today's economic system in the region. First, the whole of Finnmark is highly developed and modernized, not lagging behind the rest of the country in this respect. This is for example seen clearly in the reindeer herding, which has been heavily mechanized – and com-mercialized – in recent years. Second, throughout the centuries the originally exclusive Sami territories have been penetrated by many other groups of settlers, with different ethnic and cultural roots, in the long run turning the Sami into a minority in the county as a whole, though the Sami still are in a clear majority in the inland "Sami core areas" of Finnmark. There are Norwegian settlements on the coast with a continuous history of several hundred years, as there have been generations of Kvens in many inland and fjord habitations. Even if these groups obviously are not in the position to claim indigenous rights, as the Sami indisputably are, it cannot be contested that they are holders of some kinds of customary rights.

Thus the spatial history of Finnmark has other factors at play than does, for example, Canada. In addition, the restricted size of the territory in question creates problems for any model of rights distribution and management. With its 48,000 square kilometres, Finnmark is tiny compared to other areas in which land tenure issues are in question today, as in Canada and Australia. In Finnmark there is no longer space for expansion. There is no frontier left.

These observations may provide some explanation as to why the status of Sami rights today seems confusing and even paradoxical, and why authorities and politicians obviously experience dilemmas. On the one hand, the last decade has seen laws and international conventions that secure for the Sami the status of an indigenous people in Norway. On the other hand, the issue of Sami land rights – seen as fundamental for the future of Sami life and culture –

remain to be settled. To date, two important rights have been juridically stated, namely, language rights and political rights, though it should be added that the Sami Parliament in most cases has been granted only an advisory capacity. It remains to be seen whether the authorities will take the decisive step and accept economic and exclusive land tenure rights for the only indigenous people in the Nordic world.

1   In the inter-war period, after the Finnish declaration of independence in 1917, the Greater Finland (Suur-Suomi) movement, which appealed to expatriated Finns as well as to Finnish nationals scared the Norwegian authorities no less than "Fennomania" had. Hence the expression "the Finnish menace" became a strong rhetoric element in the political and diplomatic vocabulary well into the inter-war period, even if the official Norwegian enemy picture of Finland rather belonged to the clandestine world of politics and diplomacy (Eriksen & Niemi 1981).

References:

Andersen, A. 1989. *Sii'daen som forsvant. Østsamene i Pasvik etter den norsk-russiske grensetrekning i 1826,* Kirkenes, Sør-Varanger Museum.

Berg, R. 1994. *Norsk utenrikspolitikks historie,* Doctoral thesis, University of Bergen, Bergen.

Bergsland, K. 1994. *Bidrag til sydsamenes historie,* Centre of Sami Studies, University of Tromsø, Tromsø.

Bjørklund, I. 1985. *Fjordfolket i Kvænangen. Fra samisk samfunn til norsk utkant 1550-1980,* Tromsø/Oslo/Bergen/Stavanger, Norwegian University Press.

Brantenberg, T. 1985. "The Alta-Kautokeino Conflict, Saami Reindeer Herding and Ethnopolitics," Brøsted, J. & al. (eds.), *Native Power,* Bergen/Oslo/Stavanger/Tromsø, Norwegian University Press.

Brantenberg, T. 1991. "Constructing indigenious self-government in a nation state: Samediggi - the Sami Parliament in Norway," Jull P. & Roberts, S. (eds.), *The Challenge of the Northern Regions,* Darwin, Australian National University, North Australia Research Unit: 66-128.

Brantenberg, T. 1995. "Murky Agenda in the Mørketid: Norwegian Policy, Sami Politics and the Tromsø Conference," Brantenberg T., Hansen, J. & Minde, H. (eds.) *Becoming Visible. Indigenous Politics and Self-Government,* Centre for Sami Studies, University of Tromsø: 27-38.

Bratrein, H. D. 1984. "Fra samisk "overhøyhet" til norsk i Tromsen led på 14/1500-tallet," *Acta Borealia:* 25-46.

Brox, O., 1984. Nord-Norge: *Fra allmenning til koloni,* Oslo, Norwegian University Press.

Dellenbrant, J. Å. & Olsson, M.O. (eds.) 1994. *The Barents Region. Security and Economic Development in the European North,* Umeå, CERUM.

Drivenes, E. A. 1985 I. "Historie med store bokstaver" *Nytt norsk tidsskrift,* Norwegian University Press: 83-85.

Drivenes. E. A. 1985 II. *Fiskarbonde og gruveslusk,* Oslo, Norwegian University Press.

Drivenes, E. A. 1992. "Religion, Church and Ethnic Minorities in Norway up to 1940," Kerr, D. (ed.), *Religion, State and Ethnic Groups. Governments and Non-dominant Ethnic Groups in Europe, 1850-1940.* Vol. II, New York/-Darthmouth, New York University Press: 205-228.

Drivenes, E. A. & Jernsletten, R. 1994. "Det gjenstridige Nord-Norge. Religiøs, politisk og etnisk mobilisering" Drivenes, E.-A., Hauan, M. A. & Wold, H. (eds.), *Nordnorsk kulturistorie,* Vol. I, Oslo, Gyldendal: 210-279.

Eidheim, H. 1985. "Indigenous Peoples and the State: The Saami Case in Norway" Brøsted, J. & al. (eds.), *Native Power,* Bergen/Oslo/Stavanger/Tromsø, Norwegian University Press: 155-171.

Eriksen, G. 1993. *Alders tids bruk,* Oslo/Tromsø/Bergen, Norwegian University Press.

Eriksen, K.E. 1991. "Norwegian and Swedish Educational Policies vis-à-vis Non-dominant Ethnic Groups" Tomiac, J. (ed.), *Schooling, Educational Policy and Ethnic Identity. Comparative Studies on Governments and Non-dominant Ethnic Groups in Europe, 1850-1940,* Vol. I., New York/Darthmouth, New York University Press.

Eriksen, K. E. & Niemi, E. 1981. *Den finske fare. Sikkerhetsproblemer og minoritetspolitikk i nord 1860-1940,* Oslo/Bergen/Tromsø, Norwegian University Press: 63-86.

81

Fulsås, N. 1986. "Husholdsøkonomi og kapitalistisk økonomi i Nordland, 1850-1950" *Historisk tidsskrift*, Oslo, Norwegian University Press: 28-52.

Hansen, L. I. 1984. "Trade and Markets in Northern Fenno-Scandinavia AD. 1550-1750" *Acta Borealia*, Oslo, Novus: 47-79.

Hansen, L. I. 1986. *Samiske rettigheter til jord på 1600-tallet. "Finnejorder" i Sør-Troms*, Oslo, Tromsø Museums skrifter, Vol. XX, Novus.

Hansen, L. I. 1990. *Handel i nord. Samiske samfunnsendringer ca. 1550 - ca. 1700*, Doctoral thesis, University of Tromsø, Tromsø

Haarstad, K. 1981. *Samiske vandringer i Sør-Norge*, Trondheim, Tapir.

Haarstad, K. 1992. *Sørsamisk historie: Ekspansjon og konflikter i Rørostraktene*, Trondheim, Tapir.

Jernsletten, R. 1986 a. "The Land Sales Act of 1902 as a Means of Norwegianization," *Acta Borealia:* 3-20.

Jernsletten, R. 1986 b. *Samebevegelsen i Norge. Idé og strategi 1900-1940*, Dissertation, Universitetet i Tromsø, Tromsø.

Jokipii, M. 1982. "Finsk bosetting i Nord-Norge - historiske hovedlinjer," Kalhama, M. L. (ed.), *Finnene ved Ishavets strender,* Turku, The Migration Institute: 19-71.

Jull, P. 1995. "Through a Glass Darkly: Scandinavian Sami Policy in Foreign Perspective" in Brantenberg, T., Hansen, J. & Minde, H. (eds.) *Becoming Visible. Indigenous Politics and Self-Government,* Centre for Sami Studies, University of Tromsø, Tromsø: 129-140.

Korpijaakko-Labba, K. 1994. *Om samernas rättsliga ställning i Sverige-Finland,* Helsinki, Juristförbundets förlag.

Minde, H. 1980. "Samebevegelsen, Det norske arbeiderparti og samiske rettigheter," Thuen, T. (ed.), *Samene - urbefolkning og minoritet*, Oslo/Tromsø/Bergen, Norwegian University Press: 87-111.

Minde, H. 1991. "Ei politisk handling i normal tyding av ordet?" Samerettsforskningen i et hundreår," *Historisk tidskrift*, Oslo, Norwegian University Press: 539-565.

Minde, H. 1992. *Samenes historie som etterkrigshistorisk forskningsfelt*, Etterkrigshistorisk Register, no. 18. LOS, Bergen

Minde, H. 1993. "A century of Norwegian Research into Sami rights," *Scandinavian Studies in Law*, Vol. 37, Stockholm, Juristföreningens förlag: 109-140.

Minde, H. 1994. "Den samepolitiske mobiliseringens vekst og fall fra ca. 1900-1940," Sørensen, Ø. (ed.), *Nasjonal identitet - et kunstprodukt?,* NFR, Oslo: 113-138.

Minde, H. 1995. "The International Movement of Indigenous Peoples: an Historical Perspective" in Brantenberg, T., Hansen, J. & Minde, H. (eds.), *Becoming visible. Indigenous Politics and Self-Government,* Centre for Sami Studies, University of Tromsø, Tromsø: 9-26.

Nielsen, J. P. 1991. "Ønsket tsaren seg en isfri havn i nord," *Historisk tidsskrift,* Oslo, Norwegian University Press: 606-621.

Nielsen, J. P. 1992. "Den norske trussel." Et lite kjent aspekt ved de russisk-norske forbindelser 1826-1917," Niemi, E. (ed.), *Pomor. Nord-Norge og Nord-Russland gjennom tusen år,* Oslo, Gyldendal: 53-68.

Nielssen, A.R. 1986. "Economic Adaption among the Coast Sami Population in Finnmark c. 1700," *Acta Borealia:* 21-42.

Nielssen, A.R. 1994. "The Importance of the Hanseatic Trade for the Norwegian Settlement in Finnmark," in Henn, V. & Nedkvitne, A. (eds.), *Norwegen und die Hanse,* Peter Lang: 19-30.

Niemi, E. 1977. *Oppbrudd og tilpassing,* Vadsø, Vadsø kommune.

Niemi, E. 1983. *Vadsøs historie,* Vol. I., Vadsø, Vadsø kommune.

Niemi, E. 1992 a. "The Kvens in Vadsoe, Northern Norway, 1850-1940" Engman, M. (ed.), *Ethnic Identity in Urban Europe. Comparative Studies on Governments and Non-dominant Ethnic Groups in Europe, 1850-1940,* Vol. VIII. New York/Darthmouth, New York University Press: 131-158.

Niemi, E. (ed.) 1992 b. *Pomor. Nord-Norge og Nord-Russland gjennom tusen år,* Oslo, Gyldendal.

Niemi, E. 1994 a. "Den lange, lange sti over myrene og ind i skogene. Hvem har traaket op den?" Drivenes, E.-A., Hauan, M.A. & Wold, H.A. (eds.), *Nordnorsk kulturhistorie,* Vol. I, Oslo, Gyldendal: 119-131.

Niemi, E. 1994 b. "Østsamene - ressursutnyttelse og rettigheter," NOU 1994:21: *Bruk av land og vann i Finnmark i historisk perspektiv. Bakgrunnsmateriale for Samerettsutvalget:* 299-350.

Niemi, E. 1995 a. "The Finns in Northern Scandinavia and Minority Policy," Tägil, S. (ed.), *Ethnicity and Nation Building in the Nordic World,* Hurst & Co, London: 145-178.

Niemi, E. 1995 b. "Nation-building, Regionalism and West-European Culture: Northern Scandinavia 1850-1950," *Europa und Norden,* NFR, Oslo: 40-50.

Niemi, E. 1995 c. "The Pomor Trade from a Norwegian Perspective," *Way North. The Barents Region.* University of Tromsø, Tromsø Museum: 26-36.

Niemi, E. 1995 d. "History of Minorities: The Sami and the Kvens" in Hubbard, W.H., Myhre, J.E., Nordby, T. & Songer, S. (eds.), *Making a Historical Culture. Histography in Norway.* Scandinavian University Press, Oslo/Copenhagen/Stockholm/Boston: 325-346.

Odner, K. 1992. *The Varanger Saami. Habitation and Economy AD 1200-1900,* Oslo, Scandinavian University Press.

NOU 1984:18. *Om samenes rettsstilling*

NOU 1993:34. *Rett til og forvaltning av land og vann i finnmark. Bakgrunnsmateriale for Samerettsutvalget*

NOU 1994:21. *Bruk av land og vann i Finnmark i historisk perspektiv. Bakgrunnsmateriale for Samerettsutvalget*

Pedersen, S. 1994. "Bruken av land og vann i Finnmark inntil første verdenskrig," NOU 1994:21. *Bruk av land og vann i Finnmark i historisk perspektiv. Bakgrunnsmateriale for Samerettsutvalget.*

NOU 1997: *4. Naturgrunnlaget for samisk kultur.*

NOU 1997: *5. Urfolks landrettigheter etter folkerett og utenlandsk rett. Bakgrunnsmateriale for Samerettsutvalget.*

Sandvik, G. 1980. "Ei forelda lære: Statens umatrikulerte grunn i Finnmark" Thuen, T. (ed.), *Samene - urbefolkning og minoritet.* Oslo/Bergen/Tromsø, Norwegian University Press: 50-61.

Sandvik, G. 1993 I. "Statens grunn i Finnmark. Et historisk perspektiv," NOU 1993:34. *Rett til og forvaltning av land og vann i Finnmark. Bakgrunnsmateriale for Samerettsutvalget.*

Sandvik, G., 1993 II. "The Non-existent Sami Language Rights in Norway," Vilfan, S. (ed.), *Ethnic Groups and Language Rights. Comparative Studies on Governments and Non-dominant Ethnic Groups in Europe, 1850-1940,* Vol. III. New York/Darthmouth, New York University Press: 269-290.

Stokke, O.S. & Tunander, O. (eds.) 1994. *The Barents Region. Cooperation in the Arctic Europe.* Oslo/London/New Delhi, Sage Publications.

Sæther, O. 1992. "Nordmenn på Murmanskkysten," Niemi, E. (ed.), *Pomor. Nord-*

Norge og Nord-Russland gjennom tusen år, Oslo, Gyldendal: 69-84.

Thuen, T. (ed.) 1980. *Samene – urbefolkning og minoritet,* Oslo/Bergen/Tromsø, Norwegian University Press.

Thuen, T. 1995. *Quest for Equity. Norway and the Saami Challenge,* St. John's, ISER, Memorial University of Newfoundland.

Tønnesen, S. 1972/1979. *Retten til jorden i Finnmark.* Bergen/Oslo/Tromsø, Norwegian University Press.

Vorren, Ø. 1989. "Veidekulturens arealfordeling, siidagrenser og ressursutnytting i Samelands nordøstlige strøk," Aarset, B. (ed.), *Grenser i Sameland,* Oslo, Samiske Samlinger Vol. XIII, Norsk folkemuseum: 12-42.

Wikan, S. 1995 *Grensebygda Neiden. Møte mellom folkegrupper og kampen om ressursene,* Stonglandseidet, Nordkalottforlaget.

Nils Jernsletten[1]

Sami Traditional Terminology:

*Professional Terms Concerning Salmon,
Reindeer and Snow*

1 Traditional knowledge

The term "traditional knowledge" here refers to that knowledge which is acquired and preserved through generations in an original or local society. This knowledge consists of experience in working to secure a subsistence from nature. Observations are tied to being able to understand phenomena and connections in nature, so that people will be able to use nature for sustenance. This knowledge can be said to be usage-oriented. The Sami language(s) has(have), for example, words for grasses and plants which have been used as foodstuffs, and which have been important in the grazing of live-stock, cattle and reindeer. But there are few terms for flowering plants which, though quite visible in the summer landscape, are nevertheless not useful. Likewise there are few names for small birds, and of these names many are compounds words combining a modifier with *cizáš* (small bird, sparrow). At the same time there is a richer vocabulary having to do with sea and waterfowl, which have been useful as food sources.

The Sami have to this day maintained a hunting/gathering tradition that is thousands of years old. Modern reindeer herding represents a relatively new development over the last four hundred years, but today it is this very reindeer herding culture which has best preserved the hunter/gatherers' ways of using the environment. Hunting and fishing have been important secondary modes of production. Therefore, most of the inherited knowledge about landscape, weather, climate and animal life has been preserved. The prerequisite for transmission of this knowledge to subsequent generations is that the language has exact expressions and precise terms for those concepts which are important for exploiting nature's possibilities to support life. Based on this usage, a vocabulary and a wealth of fixed expressions about conditions in nature and animal life is developed which mirrors human activity. The vocabulary consists of specialized terms, an example of which is *čearru* (flat highland area with little vegetation). This is a landscape term, and the word has subsequently in western Sami dialects come to mean both the landscape and the group using the landscape – in other words, it has come to have the same meaning as the *siida.*

Such a specificity of language also includes fixed expressions in which everyday words are given a more specialized content, so that knowing each individual word is not enough to be able to understand the expression. The expression *dán fierpmis lea boada* means "this net can bring in a good catch," whereas a word-for-word translation would read "in this net is coming."

2 *"Silent knowledge" and knowledge preserved in words and expressions*

Much of traditional knowledge is closely connected with people's personal experiences. The art of poling a riverboat in the current, of catching ptarmigan with a snare, or of catching salmon with a net can't be learned through instructions and lectures. Poling a boat is a skill that requires thorough knowledge of the currents in the river and how the boat moves in different types of currents. When one sets out to snare ptarmigan, one must have knowledge about the ptarmigan's movements and feeding habits in the landscape, how the ptarmigan behaves in different weather conditions, and knowledge of snow conditions. The hunter must be able to read the ptarmigan's tracks. The young pupil learns all this in working with an experienced hunter; through observing, experiencing, and through asking.

That which forms the basis for this knowledge is one's own observations and practical experience. The terms one learns are a rich mix of experiences and associations. As one begins to connect words and terms to one's observations and experiences, this knowledge is verbalized, systematized, committed to memory.

Term content can consist in part of a skill – for example, the verb *goargŋut* (to pole a boat) – which cannot be expanded to enable one to learn how to pole a boat. The term also includes experience and knowledge about currents, eddies, and a river boat, which can be expressed in words. The terms and knowledge, therefore, consist of a non-linguistic portion which is experienced physically, of the type: "that which you see here is called x," or "what I am doing now is called y."

The cognitive content of such traditional knowledge which can be expressed in words and expressions is deposited in language in the form of terms – "professional expressions" – with precise explanations. But the observations are limited to that which the people in the group or local society observe in their own activities, and often include little in the way of underlying explanations beyond that which can be derived from one's own observations. The salmon-fishers in Tana know a lot about the salmon's life-cycle in the river, and have terminology according to age, gender, migratory routes, whether it is a spawning salmon or a *čuonžá* (a sexually mature salmon which doesn't spawn). But, as a traditional salmon-fisher one doesn't need to know where the salmon wanders in the sea from the time it leaves the river until it returns to spawn.

The close connection between people's activities and skills and the knowledge preserved in the form of terms and words is also evident when linguistic expressions and terminology disappear alongside the disappearance of the activity with which the knowledge is connected. Pekka Sammallahti writes about this:

As a matter of fact, oral tradition does not seem to be very powerful in preserving old hunting terms (Sammallahti 1982).

As examples of knowledge which have been lost, he names old words from wild reindeer hunting which are now only known through dictionaries. As is known, the hunting of wild reindeer ended during the 1700s in Sami-inhabited areas. There is a corresponding example with seal terminology discussed below. The expression "silent knowledge" can denote both that knowledge is not preserved and also that it is not transmitted through language alone in the form of words and descriptions.

3 Transmission of knowledge

To acquire such knowledge one must partake in work together with someone older who possesses the knowledge and experience. The teacher/master doesn't give theoretical introductions in advance. The pupil must learn through trying that which he/she has observed. Depending on how eager the youth is to learn, he/she can put the observations and experiences into words. In this manner the terms are appropriated through an intensive and detailed education where the activity and the learning of terminology through language are closely connected. The insight that the next generation receives in such a manner is quite exhaustive. This is the prerequisite for preserving the knowledge for the future, since this cultural tradition isn't built on written documentation. Knowledge is transmitted through observing, learning skills, and systematizing this in linguistic expressions, terms, and professional jargon.

Stories are an important element in this "trade didactics," or manner of learning. In spare moments the salmon-fisher tells of his successful catches and uses the fisherman's professional terminology in the telling. The youth deepen their knowledge through listening and asking questions, and connect the comments to their own experiences.

4 Examples of Sami knowledge

Here we will look at some examples of Sami traditional knowledge with reference to specific terminology. The vocabulary is from Konrad Nielsons dictionary[2] unless noted otherwise, and current transcription standards are used.

4.1 Landscape, hunting terrain, fishing places

The hunter, fisherman and reindeer herder's prerequisite for making a living from nature is an intimate knowledge of the landscape. The old Sami society was organized in groups of 10 to 12 families who had their seasonal dwellings in common areas. According to the season, they moved between their fixed dwellings and hunted and fished. Within their area they knew the reindeer's migratory routes and the best hunting places, current and riverbed conditions in the salmon rivers, and fishing spots in lakes or on the fjord. Both place names and the great wealth of appellatives which designate landscape forms and bed and current conditions in rivers, lakes and fjords, are documentation of a comprehensive usage of land and water. A large vocabulary makes it possible to describe and remember landscapes and places in rivers and lakes when conversing about hunting and fishing.

4.2 Seasons, ice and snow

Professor Israel Ruong underscores the importance that snow and ice have in people's life and subsistence in the arctic and sub-arctic areas. With the proper knowledge and skill snow and ice could be used to one's advantage in hunting and in the transportation of food. Knowledge of snow was, moreover, important for the reindeer herder:

> ... snow's importance became, if possible, even greater when the wild reindeer hunters went over to reindeer herding. Winter grazing could then be decisive for the continuation of the trade. Winter grazing became one of the most important topics of discussion.

The layer of the snow, increase in thickness, consistency, changes in consistency, melting, bare ground in contrast to the snow-covered ground, all had to be expressed in a conscious linguistic form (Ruong 1964:75).

4.2.1 Grazing conditions

Grazing conditions for reindeer are naturally important for reindeer herders. There are many words which designate grazing conditions, particularly difficult conditions. These words are often characterized with "then there is poor grazing." Weather conditions during the autumn can be decisive for grazing conditions in winter. If a dry snow falls after the ground has frozen, then no layer of ice is formed over the heather and lichen and the reindeer can easily dig down to find fodder. But if a wet snow falls as the ground is in the process of freezing, then we get varying degrees of ice formation on the ground:

Seaŋas: the dry, large-grained and water-holding snow at the deepest layers, closest to the ground surface, found in late winter and spring. It is easy for reindeer to dig through *seaŋas.*

Skárta: when there has been rain, and the snow has fastened itself to the ground; a hard layer of snow on the ground. This causes poor grazing conditions.

Sarti: a layer of frozen snow on the ground below the snow layers, acting as an ice sheet. This snow formation causes poor grazing conditions.

Čuohki: an ice sheet on pastures formed by rain on open ground that subsequently freezes. This causes the worst grazing as the reindeer are unable to dig down to the lichen.

Intermittent freeze/thaw conditions and high winds that pack the snow can also cause difficult grazing conditions:

Oppas: thickly-packed snow, still allows tolerable grazing conditions if the snow is of the *luotkku (loose)* or *seaŋas* type.

Čearga: a hard-packed snow "which one can't sink one's staff into,"

formed by strong wind packing the snow into hollows and
depressions.
Činus: firm, even snow that falls in mild weather.

During spring, when the snow becomes wet throughout, wind and
freezing can make the snow pack tight and hard, *ceavvi*. Later in the
spring, during the *bievla*-phase, the hard snow packs *čearga* and
ceavvi become *jassa,* snowdrifts or snow fields.

The effect of reindeer and humans on the snow pack also has an
impact on grazing conditions. Both *čiegar,* a snow field where
reindeer have passed, and *fieski,* where a reindeer herd has grazed,
can freeze so that *čilvi* is created. *Šalka* and *šalkačiegar,* where
humans or reindeer have passed, can freeze to a hard layer of snow
or ice. But if new snow, *vahca* or *luotkku,* falls on *čilvi,* this can
through sublimation and pressure form *seaŋas* so that grazing conditions improve. Israel Ruong refers to a description of the *čiegar*-
hunt from the writings of Johannes Tornæus: when difficult snow
conditions were such that the reindeer kept gathered together, the
Sami searched out a *čiegar* and set up snares around the reindeer
herd during the night. In the morning they sent in their dogs to
frighten the reindeer into the snares (Ruong 1964:86).

4.2.2 Traveling and snow (skiing) conditions

Snow conditions have been an important factor for both the hunter
and the reindeer herder. A number of words describe snow conditions in relationship to travel:

jodádat: smooth skiing conditions.
dobádat: sticky skiing conditions.
doavdnji: so much snow that skis, sleighs and sledges don't reach
down to the ground; snow which falls on hard snow.
sabet-doavdnji, reahka-doavdnji: compound-words – "ski-snow" and
"sledge-snow."

Above are described some types of snow formations in different situations. Many more can be described: snow types; travel conditions on ice; winter, spring and summer phases of snow; ice phases on lakes and rivers; the effect of reindeer on snow layers; and snow formation from drifting, to mention the most important. The word list provided at the end of this article lists many of the precise Sami terms for different ice and snow conditions.

4.2.3 Tracks

In providing excellent conditions for tracking, snow has been of great help to hunters, and the Sami language has developed rich terminology in this areas as well:

> *áinnahas, -hasa:*[3] untouched, i.e. without tracks, snow (Jernsletten 1994, hereafter <nj>).
> *doalli, doali:* winter road or track covered by snow but still distinguishable.
> *jodáhat, -haga:* track in the snow left by a migrating reindeer herd.
> *jolas, jollasa:* tracks made in the snow by reindeer, dogs or wolves which have gone in single file.
> láhttu, láhtu: ski track.
> márahat, -haga: large, beaten winter track.
> ulahat, ulahaga: almost unrecognizable winter trail or track that is snowed under or covered with drift snow.

4.3 Knowledge of the reindeer possessed by reindeer hunters and herdsmen

It is well known that the Sami language has a very large and nuanced vocabulary for reindeer. Much of this nuanced terminology has its origin in traditional forms of hunting and is well-described in Nils Isak Eira's *Boazobargi giella* (Reindeer herders' language). In the preface (Eira 1984:2) Eira underscores the importance of registering this vocabulary and the knowledge it contains, especially in light of the fact that herding practices and organization now are in a process of change, as the children of today no longer participate in and learn the fundamental knowledge of the trade.

For a reindeer owner it will often be necessary to describe a reindeer so precisely that the experienced listener knows with certainty what kind of reindeer is being discussed even though those conversing do not see the animal. This applies, for example, when herds have combined or when one has lost an animal. This requires precise terms for distinct categories in order to be able to identify individuals among a large number of animals. The chart below shows the precision of Sami reindeer terminology:[4]

Figur 1
The numbers in the colums age/sex refers to age.

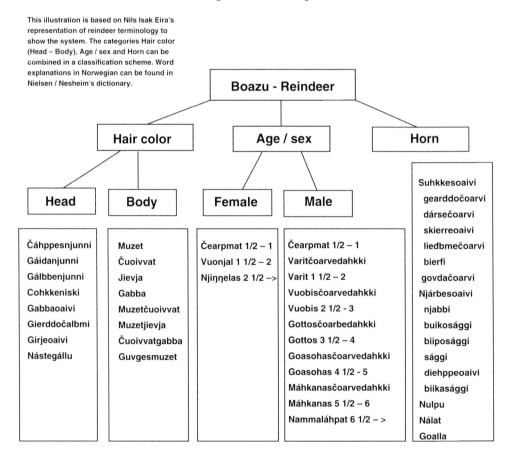

This illustration is based on Nils Isak Eira's representation of reindeer terminology to show the system. The categories Hair color (Head – Body), Age / sex and Horn can be combined in a classification scheme. Word explanations in Norwegian can be found in Nielsen / Nesheim's dictionary.

Boazu - Reindeer

Hair color | **Age / sex** | **Horn**

Head | **Body** | **Female** | **Male** | Suhkkesoaivi

Head	Body	Female	Male	Horn
Čáhppesnjunni	Muzet	Čearpmat 1/2 – 1	Čearpmat 1/2 – 1	Suhkkesoaivi
Gáidanjunni	Čuoivvat	Vuonjal 1 1/2 – 2	Varitčoarvedahkki	gearddočoarvi
Gálbbenjunni	Jievja	Njiŋŋelas 2 1/2 –>	Varit 1 1/2 – 2	dársečoarvi
Cohkkeniski	Gabba		Vuobisčoarvedahkki	skierreoaivi
Gabbaoaivi	Muzetčuoivvat		Vuobis 2 1/2 - 3	liedbmečoarvi
Gierddočalbmi	Muzetjievja		Gottosčoarbedahkki	bierfi
Girjeoaivi	Čuoivvatgabba		Gottos 3 1/2 – 4	govdačoarvi
Nástegállu	Guvgesmuzet		Goasohasčoarvedahkki	Njárbesoaivi
			Goasohas 4 1/2 - 5	njabbi
			Máhkanasčoarvedahkki	buikosággi
			Máhkanas 5 1/2 – 6	biiposággi
			Nammaláhpat 6 1/2 – >	sággi
				diehppeoaivi
				biikasággi
				Nulpu
				Nálat
				Goalla

4.4 Knowledge about river salmon

Salmon fishing has always been an important part of Sami subsistence along the fjords and large rivers. The Sami have gathered and passed on knowledge from generation to generation about the salmon's life cycle in fjords or rivers, about the salmon's behavior from the time that it goes up the river in spring and establishes itself in a fixed area until spawning time. The fisherman must be familiar with bed and current conditions in the river in order to know where the good fishing spots are. Hans Henriksen, who grew up along the Deatnu/Tana River, Finnmark's largest river, famous for its salmon fishing, tells of fishing salmon with weirs, a system of fixed nets:

> When one wishes to find a suitable place for a weir, one must look for a *joddosadji* (bag-net place). At the place where the bag-net will be the river bed must slope a little outwards and down. If the *joddosadji* doesn't have the right even slope outwards and downwards, the salmon won't go into the bag-net (Henriksen 1945).

This excerpt shows what kind of thorough knowledge the salmon fisher must have about river, current and riverbed conditions, and about the behavior of salmon in the river. Salmon fishers in Deatnu/Tana have a rich vocabulary which designates deep or shallow water, still places or currents and strength, etc. Here are some examples from that terminology:

Words for deep water:

> *áhparas:* very deep place in the water.
> *jorbmi:* deep place, pool, in a river (open hole in a bog).
> *oalli:* the main channel of a river.
> *fávli:* the water far out, the deep water; the deep part of a river; the part near the middle of a fjord (where it is deepest).

Words for shallow water:

coagis: shallow, shallow place.
cohkolat: shallow place in the sea, in a lake or river; pond or sound which is dry in summer.
njuorra: shoal, shallow, in the sea or in a lake; fishing bank.
suohpa: shallow place where a river can be crossed.

Words for quietly flowing water:

dappal: short stretch of smooth water between rapids in a river; large deep pool (also in a rapid, near shore) with backwater.
doažži (adj): still flowing, with little current: currentless water.
fielbmá: small, slow river of even depth; slow, deep place in a (small) river.
goatnil: still water, without any current, near the bank or by a stone in a river.
savu: smoothly flowing stretch of water in a big river.

Words for current, strength, rapids and falls:

besko: strong counter-current in a river.
borsi: lit. 'cauldron fall' (of a waterfall surrounded by sheer mountain walls on three sides), now only used as a proper name of a river.
boršu: eddy (white) in rapids
gorži: waterfall.
guoika: rapids.
guorvil: rough rapids, in which the water breaks and "foams" over the rocks; a small waterfall which a boat can navigate going upstream.
geavŋŋis: big rapids with falls in a large river (impossible or difficult to navigate in a boat).
njavvi: small rapids in a river.
njielahat: whirlpool, in which the river draws down anything that comes in its path.
njearri: a shallow and comparatively large njavvi.
rohči: narrowing, narrow, contracted portion of a river (with strong current or rapids) or valley.

Beaŋgil refers to an old, now illegal, fishing method and derives from a proper name designating a jointly owned place for netting salmon in the Karasjok River above the site of the church.

Knowledge of the salmon's life in the river is reflected in a rich vocabulary about salmon according to age and important age classes:

> *diddi:* a small male salmon, up to 2.5 kg which swims up the Tana river later than other salmon.
> *lindor:* a small male salmon, larger than *diddi.*
> *goadjin:* large male salmon.
> *duovvi:* roe salmon.
> *čuonžá:* fatty salmon which has neither roe nor semen, swims up the river in the autumn.
> *vuorru:* "winter steady" salmon which remains in the river throughout the winter.
> *šoaran:* a vuorru which goes down to the sea in the spring and returns again in the autumn.

The fat salmon *čuonžá* and the *guvžá* (sea trout) come up-river so late in the autumn that due to regulations of the fishing seasons fishing them is now prohibited in Norway. Both *čuonžá* and *guvžá* are fatty fish which people used to net during late summer and autumn.[5]

4.5 Lost knowledge – seal terminology

Knowledge which is preserved as professional jargon in oral tradition can be lost when work methods and lifestyles change. The original rich Sami terminology concerning seals is partially forgotten, as seal hunting has lost its significance as a form of subsistence in Sami areas. Sami classification of seals according to species, age and gender, as well as other criteria, appears to have been as specific as that for reindeer herding. Some terms for seal are to be found in Knud Leem's dictionaries, but the definitions are poor. In Nils V. Stockfleth's dictionary there are a number of words under the heading "seal," though the meanings are not given:

buosste, dullja, dulsenjunne, dællja, fattenjunne, havdagas, hav-skargubbo, jorbboairre, jæges, njafco, oiddo, riekko, ruovdagas, rædde, and *vadnel:* a group of seals. The generic, non-specific word for seal is *njuorjo.* Professor Asbjørn Nesheim has designated explanations for a few seal terms, such as: *ainne* (female seal), *af'čo* (full-grown female), *dævok* (full-grown male), *gætte* (ring seal), *luos'te* (yearling), *nuorroš* (stone seal: Phoca vitulina), *roahkka* (full-grown male), *skavddo* (yearling), *vjæfse* (not yet a year old, but weaned).

5 Transmission of such knowledge in today's society

5.1 On knowledge and learning

The prerequisite for transmitting knowledge to the next generation in the old Sami society was that children were together with their parents in work situations where they followed along and heard adult conversations. The young took part early on in the adults' tasks, and received a gradual introduction to professional knowledge together with training in professional skills. With personal experience in the work they could understand and participate in the conversations and stories of knowledgeable adults during free moments, and in this way they could broaden their terminology and knowledge.

A central concern of reindeer-herding Sami is that their children are taken away from work in reindeer herding when they enter the Norwegian school system and thus are not exposed to an important introduction to the knowledge that is necessary for one who one day will become a reindeer owner or herder himself/herself. Even though Sami authorities today have greater opportunities possibility than previously to adapt school curriculum to the needs and wishes of Sami society, schools in Sami villages are also typically Norwegian and European in that they are markedly *theoretical.* The majority of what Sami children learn is in the classroom, with the help of pedagogic instructional material. Every pedagogue knows that the instructional method isn't just an outward pedagogical form, but that the method informs the content. What this means is that an important portion of the content of the Sami traditional knowledge is lost when the type of insight and understanding is taken away which is tied to a physical approach and experience together with an introduction to and expansion of terminology.

I imagine that a good deal of knowledge appropriation in modern physical science takes place with demonstrations, exercises and practice in laboratories and fieldwork out in nature, and that learning is unimaginable without this practice. The "laboratories" of the Sami and other small societies have been the landscape, the sea, rivers and lakes where the youth have practiced and learned. Modern educational methods cannot fully replace this older manner of learning. If scholastic instruction is not supplemented with instruction in the environment where the knowledge belongs, that is, in nature itself, important aspects of that knowledge will be lost. In this sense "Sami"- schools are Sami in name only and are European in content.

5.2 Sami knowledge for the future

I have named some aspects of the transmission of knowledge in today's educational society where traditional Sami knowledge hasn't received a place. This applies also to Sami society. As important as it is to describe what doesn't work, it is naturally just as important to try to find out how we can activate the old knowledge as a living part of the Sami society of the future. Paradoxically, we can perhaps take inspiration from some of the most modern trends in the high-status areas of industrial and informational society. There one finds expensive alternative courses for over-stressed leaders. An important component in such courses is typically "survival tech-niques" in strenuous conditions. Here the participants must be out in nature and "survive," and they must "learn" simple fragments of nature-knowledge, such as useful plants, weather and climate, and ice and snow. Here there is an interest in that which we in our context call "indigenous peoples' knowledge" or "traditional knowledge," and for mountain people's survival techniques. Sami knowledge thereby has "status" in such contexts.

In elementary schools in some Sami villages there are courses in "the field" of local knowledge and work skills, and there have been summer courses in the mountains in so-called reindeer herding Sami areas (or schools). But in order to create a solid foundation for this instruction a subject area must be developed at the secondary school, college and university levels. Also here we have an example from the south which we can expand upon. In the subject of ecology at the Zoological Institute at the University of Oslo, the researchers Ivar Mysterud and Eivind Østbye have lectured in snow and ice with the use of Sami terminology. The foundation for the use of Sami terminology was established through a research project on Sami ice and snow terminology.

The material discussed in chapter *4.2 Seasons and snow* was collected and handled in a project undertaken by the *Sámi Instituhtta* in Guovdageaidnu, and which was developed through the initiative of Eivind Østbye and Ivar Mysterud at the Zoological Institute, University of Oslo. The two performed a functional analysis of the words and created a schematic representation of snow packing and succession. Nils Jernsletten at the Institute for Languages and Literature at the University of Tromsø was responsible for the philological portion of the project, and Nils Isak Eira conducted the interviews in Guovdageaidnu in November, 1975.

Our experience from this project is that cooperation between people from different fields is necessary when the traditional vocabulary is to be systematized according to scientific needs and methods. Already in the registration phase it is important that the questions are developed according to criteria from different fields of study.

Sami researchers still have access to "the old knowledge" through people who have grown up and lived with traditional modes of production and who have learned from their parents in a traditional manner. It is self-evident that they must transmit their knowledge through their own language, Sami. For use in schools this knowledge must in part be transformed and re-written to the media of our time, such as writing, pictures and film. But it is very important to remember that the use of modern media cannot replace learning combined with practice.

6. Closing comments

The reader naturally understands that the description I have given of traditional Sami knowledge doesn't give insight into that knowledge. I have tried to describe it in such a way that we can become more aware of how this form of knowledge can be preserved and transmitted to later generations. For us Sami this will have its own value. For the rest of the world the old Sami knowledge can perhaps lead to an increase in respect for indigenous cultures and add a new dimension to theory-based knowledge.

Appendix

Sami vocabulary on snow and ice

aškkas, aškasa s = rough sheet of ice (esp. on a road or at the foot of a rock)
áhtán, áhtána s = ice on salt water
áinnádat, -daga s = surface (with newfallen snow) upon which fresh tracks are easily seen
áinnahas,-hasa s = untouched surface on snow (without tracks) <nj>
baldu, balddu s = large block of ice, ice-floe
bearta, beartta s = heavy going because the ground is bare (without snow)
bieggagaikkohat, -haga s = a place where the wind has blown the

snow away

bihci, bizi s = rime (frost)

boara, boarraga s = having smooth ice on it in spring, after the snow has melted

bodas, boddasa s = brash-ice at bottom of (shallow) river in autumn; damming up of river caused by such ice

bohkolat, -laga s = deep snow of varying depth; small (steep) snow-drift on road or where one goes (plur.: wave-like little (steep) snow drifts)

bulži, bulžži s = compact crust, coating of ice, esp. on implements

ceavvi, ceavi s = hard, compact snow

cuokca, cuovcca s = ice-bridge or snow-bridge over a river; narrow strip of ice between two lanes

cuoŋu, cugŋo (cuonju, cudnjo) s = strong crust on snow

čađgi, čađggi s = drizzle; snow thinly

čahki, čagi s = hard lump of snow (e.g. under horse's hoof), hard snowball

časttas, častasa s = hard snowdrift (smaller than *skálvi*)

čearga, čeargga s = snowdrift which is so hard that it bears; crust of snowdrift

čiegar, čiehkara s = snowfield which has been trampled and dug up by reindeer (or sheep in autumn) feeding there

činus, čitnosa s = firm, even snow (but not firm enough to bear)

čoddi, čodi s = coating of ice formed by frozen rain or sleet on stones or trees

čuohki, čuogi s = ice-crust on pasture

čuorpmas, čuorbmasa s = hail

doalli, doali s = winter road or track covered by snow but still distinguishable

doavdnji, doavnnji s = snow of such a depth that skis, or a sleigh will not come in contact with the ground; snow which falls upon hard going; *savet-doavdnji, reahka-doavdnji* = ski-d., sleigh-d.

dobádat, -daga s = sticky snow; heavy, wet snow

earbmi, earpmi s = snow consisting of very small flakes

102

fáska, fáskka s = snow blown together by the wind, snowdrift (of snow blown along the ground)

fieski, fieskki s = area where a grazing herd of reindeer has been. In winter the *fieski* stretches as far as one can see tracks of reindeer, including both the *čiegar* and parts where there is no pasturage

gállji, gálji (gálja) s = bare ice; smooth ice; very slippery going, frozen, slippery surface

geardni, geartni s = thin crust on snow

girrat adj = heavy (of the going in frosty weather, especially when there has been a hard frost after a fall of snow) (cf *sabádat*)

goahpálat, -laga s = the kind of snowstorm in which the snow falls thickly and sticks to things,(it becomes *dobádat* <nj>)

goarveskálvi s = a very big, overhanging snowdrift (cf. *skálvi*) <nj>

guovla, guovlla s = overhanging snowdrift; overhanging crag (cf *goapma, goarvi*)

jassa, jasa s = patch of snow in summer or late spring; snowdrift which is larger than *skálvi*

jiehkki, jiehki s = glacier

jiekŋa, jieŋa s = ice

jieŋkk-gávli, -gávlli s = ice along the shore of open water (the sea or rapids)

joavga, joavgga s = snow which is blown together by the wind, behind rocks or trees, but before it gets hard as *čearga*

joavgga, joavgama s = deep snow which lies undisturbed, does not get blown away (in a wood or other place where there is shelter from the wind)

joavggahat, -haga s = place where the snow lies particularly deep after snow

jođádat,-daga s = good going, .. (when the sleigh or skis run well)

jođáhat, -haga s = track in the snow left by a migrating reindeer herd

jolas, jollasa s = tracks made in the snow by reindeer, dogs or wolves which have travelled in a line

lavki, lavkki s = slippery going; ice covered with loose, dry snow with no foothold, cf. *coakci* (cf. *njuohpa, gálja*)

láhttu, láhtu s = ski-track

loanjis, loatnjása s = tracks of the whole herd of reindeer (both in winter and in summer)

luotkku, lutko s = loose snow

márahat, -haga s = large, beaten winter-track

moarádat,-daga s = the kind of going there is when the frozen surface of the snow does not bear, the kind of snow which has not a hard enough surface to bear

moaráhat s = 1) lane of water where the ice is broken up; place where a layer of ice above thicker ice is broken up, 2) plur.: pieces of ice in a lane

moarri, moari s = brittle crust of snow (thicker than *geardni*; also of frozen crust of driven snow, *čearga,* which does not quite bear; and *cuoŋu* which begis to soften becomes *moarri),* thin crust of ice (cf. *moarádat)* 2) the kind of going, surface, when the frozen snow or crust of ice breaks and cuts the legs of horses and reindeer

muohta, muohttaga s = snow

nállojiekŋa s = "needle-ice" <nj>

njáhcu, njázu s = thaw

njeađga, njeađga s = "ground-drift" (drifting snow which gets blown up from the ground) which covers road or tracks

njuohpa, njuohppaga s = slippery going, of the kind with ice under loose snow

norahat, -hagat s = pack ice (on or near a river); stretch of river-ice in autumn with uneven surface due to floating by-ice which has frozen on it; pl. also: pieces of floating ice where a boat has broken a lane in the ice

oavlluš, ovloša s = depression, hollow, with slushy snow on it, on land or on ice

ratti, ratit s = winter way made by driving reindeer (in harness) over the snow

radnu, ratnut s = tracks of a hare (on snow, where a hare has gone frequently to and fro)

ritni, rinit = (thick) rime on trees and other things (cf. *bihci*)

roavku, roavkkut s = portion of frozen water (river, lake, marsh) or frozen bank, waterside (near a spring), where the ice has formed in such a way that there is a hollow space under the top layer of ice

rodda, rotta s = hard going (too little snow)

rovda, rovdda s = weak ice which does not bear the reindeer (especially on bogs)

rudni, rutni s = ice-hole (hole for getting water or for fishing with a *juoŋas*)

ruokŋa, ruoŋa (ruotnja, ruonja) s = thin, hard crust of ice on snow

ruovdecuoŋu, -cugŋo s = "iron-crust," the hardest kind of spring (snow) crust

salggas, salgasa s = when the ice has melted away so that tools, trees etc. get free from any coating of ice <nj>

saŋas, sakŋasa (sanjas, satnjasa) s = thawed, free from ice or snow (of utensils, implements, vehicles etc.)

sarti, sartti s = a layer of frozen snow on the ground, for instance at the bottom of the snow pack, like a crust <nj>

sáissa, sáisaga s = mass of packed ice pressed up on or towards the shore

seakŋut, seaŋui (seatnjut, seanjui) v = granulate, become granulat (of snow) KN; the snow gets granulated <nj>

sealas, seallasa s = free from rime, snow or ice (of trees, forest)

sealli, seali s = melting rime on the trees

seaŋas, seakŋasa (seanjas, seatnjasa) s = granular snow at the bottom of the layer of snow

sievlla, sievlaga s = the state of things when the spring snow is so soft that one sinks in it

sievlladat, -daga s = the kind of going when one sinks in soft spring snow out of which it is difficult to lift one's foot

sittardit v = to snow very finely, with very small flakes; to drive in fine clouds, come in through cracks (of snow)

skálvi, skálvvit s = big (high, steep and usually hard) snowdrift

skárta, skártta s = thin (more or less ice-like) layer of snow frozen on to the ground

skávvi, skávi s = crust of ice on snow, formed in the evening after the sun has thawed the top of the snow during the day; thin crust which begins to form on snow, following mild weather

skilži, skilžžit s = covering of little bits of ice which hang down loosely (on rough cloth, skin with the heir on, in the hair or beard)

skoalddas, skoaldasat aj = covered with a thin, hard layer of snow

skoavddas, skoavdasat s = with an empty space, air, under it or in it (Kt only of snow)

skoavdi, skoavddi s = in spring where there is stil a thin layer of snow <nj>; KN: (Kt empty space between snow an the ground)

slievar s = IR[6]: loose, soft snow <nj>

soatma, soatmma s = ice-slush or snow-slush on the water of a river or lake

soavli, soavlli s = very wet, slushy snow, snow-slush

spildi, spilddi s = very thin layer of ice on water or milk

spoanas, spoatnasa s = 1) with a thin layer of snow on it (of ground or ice)

spoatna, spoana s = hard, firm snow to drive on (when there is little snow)

suddi, sutti s = lane, lead, hole in the ice

suohpa s = IR: a bridge of snow over a brook or a crack in a glacier <nj>

suossa, suosa s = bay ice (in river and lake; often used in plur.)

suovdnji, suovnnji s = grazing hole, hole dug by reindeer in the snow in order to feed; Kt. also of a hole in the snow where ptarmigan hide, and of a hole dug by people when getting snow for melting, or to shelter in during a storm

šalka, šalkka s = firm, hard winter way; hardtrodden snow on yard, market-place etc.

šlahttá, šlahtá s = sleet

šlavzi, šlavzzi s = wet snow, soaked; =(IR: *slab'ze*): newly fallen snow which is so wet that it does not stick to the skis <nj>

šuhči, šuži s = hard-frozen rime (on trees)

uđas, uđđasa s = avalanche

ulahat, ulahaga s = almost unrecognizable winter way, track, that is snowed under, or covered with drifted snow

vahca, vaza s = new snow; loose snow (especially new snow on the top of a layer of older snow)

veadahat, -haga s = place where snow has been blown away; (nearly) bare patch (where the wind has blown away the snow)

vuohčči s = smooth ice with moisture on top

vuojáhat, -haga s = track or way in the snow, made by vehicles or by driving a herd of reindeer.

1   All translations are provided by the author, unless otherwise noted.

2   Konrad Nielsen, Asbjørn Nesheim: *Lappisk (samisk) ordbok - Lapp dictionary,* Oslo 1979.

3   Most Sami nouns are presented in both the nominative and acc./gen. cases, as these are the two basic "root" forms for all other inflections.

4   Based on Nils Isak Eira's system of categorization of reindeer terminology. Terms can be productively combined.

5   The words above are taken from Konrad Nielsen's *Lappisk ordbok.*

6   Israel Ruong 1964.

References:

Eira, Nils Isak 1984. "Boazobargi giella," *Diedut* No. 1, Nordisk Samisk Institutt, Kautokeino.

Henriksen, Hans J. 1945. "Luossâbiw'dem jod'dobuođoin Dænost" - Laksefiske med posegarnstengsel i Tanaelva, *Festskrift til Konrad Nielsen,* Studia Septentrionalia II, Oslo: 116-129

Itkonen, T.I. 1958. *Koltan ja Kuolanlapin sanakirja I-II,* Helsinki, Suomalais-ugrilainen seura (Lexica Societatis Fenno-Ugricae).

Jernsletten, Nils Jernsletten 1994. "Tradisjonell samisk fagterminologi,"

Festskrift til Ørnulv Vorren, Tromsø Museums skrifter XXV: 234-254.

Knud Leem 1756. *En Lappisk Nomenclator efter den Dialect, som bruges af Fjeld-Lapperne i Porsanger-Fjorden,* Trondiem, Jens Christensen Winding.

Nesheim, Asbørn 1953. "Samisk seljakt og jaktabu," *Studia septentrionalia* IV, Oslo, H. Aschehoug & Co (W. Nygaard): 13-19.

Nielsen, Konrad and Asbjørn Nesheim 1979. *Lappisk (samisk) ordbok - Lapp dictionary I-V,* Oslo, Institutt for sammenlignende kulturforskning.

Roung, Israel 1964. "Jåhkåkaska sameby," Särtryck ur *Svenska Landsmål och Svenskt Folkliv.*

Sammallahti, Pekka. 1982. "Lappish (Sami) Hunting Terminology in an Historical Perspective", Åke Hulkrantz/ Ørnulv Vorren (eds.) *The Hunters, their Culture and Way of Life,* Tromsø Museums skrifter Vol XVIII, Oslo: 103-111.

Stockfleth, Nils V. 1852. *Norsk-lappisk ordbok,* Christiania.

Johan Klemet Hætta Kalstad

Aspects of Managing Renewable Resources in Sami Areas in Norway

Introduction

The Sami in Norway are usually categorized into three groups according to how they make their living. The Sea Sami – *mearra-olbmot* – live in the coastal regions in Norway. They combine fjord fishing with other livelihoods such as cattle-raising, berry-picking, etc. The *dálon* – small landholders engaged in subsistence agriculture, fresh-water fishing, berry-picking, hunting, tourism, and even keeping a small number of reindeer live in the main Sami settlement region in the northern-most parts of Fennoscandia. The third group is the *boazosápmelaččat* – the reindeer Sami – who keep semi-domesticated reindeer and engage in seasonal transhumance. Ownership of the animals in this third group is with the individual, and each owner has his/her own earmark in order to identify their animals. Something which all the Sami have in common is that they harvest renewable natural resources.

This article concentrates on the *boazosápmelaččat* – the pastoralists[1], and I shall discuss some aspects of the management of reindeer pasture land in the main Sami settlement region in Norway. I also outline the model for "co-management" of common land in some areas in the Canadian Arctic. The model is based on a formalized co-operation between aboriginal peoples and governmental agencies.[2]

Reindeer pastures

The Sami nomads move with their reindeer herds in a yearly cycle between inland pastures and the coast according to the seasonal grazing conditions. During the summer the reindeer graze on green plants and grasses along the coast, and in the wintertime they graze on lichen. The winter grazing area in the north lies inland. The inland weather is dry and cold and without significant precipitation. Thus, in the winter the inland climate does not destroy the grazing conditions with heavy snow and ice cover over the lichen, and it is possible for the reindeer to dig and find food through the snow. The migration patterns vary from area to area depending on the natural conditions, and in some parts of the reindeer areas the reindeer move in quite the opposite direction, with the winter grazing on the coast and summer grazing in the inland. This is because winters on the coast, particularly in Nordland and Trøndelag, are comparatively mild, with little snowfall as a result of the Gulf Stream.

The reindeer are not intensively managed except at critical times of the year such as calving and ear-marking, when animals are selected for harvest, and during migrations and the separating of the herds. At other times, the major human involvement consists of selecting and guiding herds to pastures.

The summer pasture land is divided into *orohat* [reindeer districts]. There are some forty districts in Finnmark County and North-Troms, the two northernmost Norwegian counties with significant reindeer herding. An *orohat* is a geographical area in which some herders have exclusive grazing rights. It is governed by its own board, which is elected annually by the herders from among themselves.

Winter pasture land is not divided into districts as is summer pasture land, and therefore the winter pastures are common land in the broad legal sense. However, each winter herd, which has been called *siida,* has its own pastures. The other herd-owners know the borders, based on traditions and "rights" in the informal sense. However, during the last couple of decades there have been changes in reindeer husbandry due to technological innovations such as snowmobiles, motorbikes, fences to prevent herds from mixing etc. As a result of this development, combined with a growing monetary economy in the north, the system of Sami reindeer production is going through a transition from subsistence-based pastoralism towards an industry integrated into a market economy. At the same time, or as a consequence of this development, the informal system does not work well. The reindeer population has increased rapidly, and in some areas overgrazing occurs.

The political objective today is to avoid overgrazing by reducing A) the number of animals and B) the number of herders. These reductions are supposed to increase 1) the weight of the animals and thus, 2) the income of the remaining herders (St.meld. nr. 28, 91-92). In order to realize these goals, reindeer husbandry is defined as a commercial activity concerned with meat production for which modern agriculture serves as a model.

The pastoralists – who are they and what are they doing

Most of the Sami pastoralists and their families live in the settlements of Guovdageaidnu/Kautokeino and Kárášjohka/Karasjok as well as in communities in Deatnu/Tana and Unjárgga/Nesseby[3]. In these villages they have their homes, and they also pay their taxes in these municipalities. The children go to school in their home towns. The pastoralists who leave the reindeer industry usually look for employment opportunities in these areas. In the inland municipalities, the reindeer industry is important, and it plays a significant role in maintaining settlement and employment.

Table 1: The population in main Sami settlement areas

	Total population		Reindeer herders	
Year	1980	1994	1980	1994
Guovdageaidnu	2963	3124	1034	1229
Kárášjohka	2649	2800	408	454
Deatnu	3335	3273	50	66
Unjárga	1086	1049	22	54

Sources: The Reindeer Offices in Guovdageaidnu and Kárášjohka and official statistics.

The coast and the coastal regions have also, however, always been an important part of pastoralism, and more than 100,000 animals are moved from the inland and to the coast every spring and about 150,000 reindeer including calves back again in the autumn.

Table 2. The number of reindeer in main settlement areas

	1980	1990	1994
Guovdageaidnu	66,100	99,300	86,500
Kárášjohka	33,800	48,500	36,200
Deatnu	6,300	7,000	6,404
Unjárga	4,500	10,400	9,900

Source: The Reindeer Offices in Kárášjohka and Guovdageaidnu.

Approximate number of reindeer in Norway:[4]

1990	1994
231,000*	206,000*

*Includes 9-10 000 reindeer in non-Sami areas in South Norway.

Source: Annual reports of Reindriftsadminstrasjon.

The circle is based on herding, and, in pursuit of a complete set of activities I put the tasks carried out within pastoralism in two

The figure below shows the herding activities annually in Guovdageaidnu:

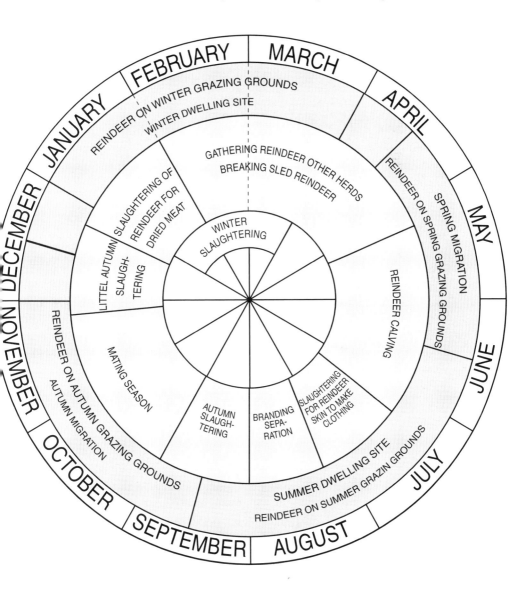

Source: *The Sami People*, 1990:173.

categories described by Paine: herding and husbandry (Paine 1964, 1994:19-32, 145-167).

Herding concerns the day to day work with the herd which consists of moving between seasonal pastures and managing the animals within the pastures. The point is to have control over *the herd of animals.* Therefore, the herder has to have contact with them on the terrain and to know where the herd is and in which direction it is moving while gathering and checking that all the animals are present. If any animals are absent, the herder has to find out where they could be and get them back to their own herd. Herding, then, includes tasks of gathering, checking and moving the animals, overseeing seasonal migrations, building and mending fences and corrals, and gathering information regarding other herds in order to avoid mixing.

Husbandry concerns *the animals in the herd* and the management of the capital in one's own herd as livestock. The family lives off its herd and takes wages from it, which means that some animals are slaughtered for sale, while the rest remain a capital asset. Selecting and making decisions as to which animals are to be slaughtered is the responsibility of husbandry. In order to be able to make decisions, the owners must have knowledge of the single animal, as it is a question of selecting a particular animal for a particular purpose and "this kind of husbandry implies constant and accurate observation of the herd by the husbander" (Paine 1964:85). If you do not know the individual animal, you can select animals for slaughter if they wear your earmark. But that means that the owner does not have knowledge of the individual animal, and it implies that the owner is about to lose control over the animals in his or her herd, even if he or she retains control over the herd of animals, i.e. that herder knows where the herd is and which direction it is moving, but he or she is not able to know the individual animal in the herd.

As mentioned above, both herding and husbandry are changing, and families do not move in same way as in previous times. All members of the family are not present at all the seasonal camps. It

114

is becoming more common for the herders to move the reindeer herds while their families stay at home, usually moving later by car directly to their summer camps. The autumn migration is done in the same way: the families travel by car, while the herders move the reindeer herds. However, the families participate in earmarking the calves in the summer and slaughtering in the autumn and winter. As a rule, the families take care of skins and antlers when the reindeer are slaughtered, as these materials are essential for making souvenirs and products which members of the families sell to tourists. For many families, tourism has become an important source of income, with tourist markets along the main roads in the coastal regions, especially those leading to North Cape which is visited by more than 200,000 persons during the few summer months. In fact, tourism has grown to be an accepted part of husbandry.

Culture as a precondition

Knowledge can be considered technology used to resolve problems and make decisions; for instance, the knowledge of how to select animals for slaughter and to avoid mixing with other herds. This knowledge is accumulated through experience and practice in daily life. However, one must recognize knowledge as something valuable. The Sami society appreciates *fitmat* [clever] as a valuable herding term which also expresses something appropriate about the herder. In husbandry, *jábálaš* [rich] is a term for being wealthy, and this wealth consists both of property and knowledge. Knowledge is a means for creating wealth while earning for the environment through the management of the circumstances. Therefore, to be jábálaš is not only a question of having a lot of animals, it is also connected with the management of your property and control over circumstances. Therefore, it is an objective to manage the herd capital in such a way as to get a *čáppa eallu* [valuable herd], which consists of good looking and productive animals (age and sex),

115

colored so as to be easily distinguishable etc. (Kalstad 1991:40-41). The language is another core of the culture, and it encapsulates and carries the values. In other words, values are embedded in the language, and these constitute *giellavuohta* [language gestalt] as an integral part of one's own surroundings (Kalstad 1994).

The villages have been the main base for the production and the preservation of values and norms. On the other hand, lack of experience and intimate knowledge of reindeer and the land lead to an extensification of herding (Beach 1990:294). In this sense, the importance of maintaining the relationship between reindeer husbandry and the Sami culture appears to be of importance. Maybe pastoralism will work without this connection, but then reindeer husbandry will become something else than a Sami industry, something more akin to commercial ranching driven by economics.

Tim Ingold has called such a radical change "Stock-rearing," and by this he means the existence of a market structure and the acceptance of commercial values (Paine 1994:189). Ingold also points out that "reindeer ranching" is becoming established in several areas in northern Scandinavia. Both pastoralism and ranching are based on grazing and livestock. However, the fundamental difference lies in land use. The pattern of land use associated with ranching is characterized by large units, extensive use of land, and extensive use of labor on the land (1980:236). When the herd no longer has intrinsic value, pastoralism will lose a great part of itself. The lack of knowledge will cause stereotyping of pastoralism.

Some of the values of Sami culture constitute the institutions which have made pastoralism possible where the natural resources have been common while the animals are privately owned; that is, a situation in which common resource and private capital occur without tragedy. In this connection I want to quote the following:

It is in the social organization of herding that pastoralism differs from conventional idea of a common pasture where everyone has free access (Bjørklund 1990:83).

I repeat that preservation of these institutions require many preconditions, and Sami culture provides the setting in which to produce, develop and rejuvenate the preconditions which serve the institutions. Therefore, an interrelation with Sami culture will maintain the reindeer industry as a form of pastoralism with its own institutions to regulate the carrying capacity of the pastures. When these institutions no longer work, problems may ensue (Bjørklund 1994:70-74). However, the linkage between pastoralism and culture nowadays is fragile, and, even in the Sami settlement areas in the inland of Finnmark, the younger pastoralists point out that they are in business just like those in other branches of primary industries.

Rights and ownership

Sami land rights have been discussed in terms of common property and private ownership. Sami rights are thus tied to the use of the land. The Sami consider the land as theirs to use, but it is more difficult for them to clarify **ownership** in terms of private or state ownership. The answer will probably be that nobody owns land, because it is **common** property and users ought to have access to it. This ambiguity concerning access rights and land usage represents a difficulty with respect to rights in the Western sense. The Sami differentiate between the right to use the land and the ownership of the land, and they assert their right to land use. It is, however, unclear what they really mean by ownership, as the question has been of little interest until the State claimed ownership of the land that the Sami had previously used without interference. In this way there is a similarity with other aboriginal peoples where the ownership and the rights to use common land are distinguished (Berkes 1994:18, Ingold 1986:223-229). The State claims to own most of the land (96 %) in Finnmark county. However, this claim has been disputed, and the issues are still undecided. The Sami Rights Committee is absorbed with the question of land ownership, and there is a great disagreement concerning this question (NOU 1993:34).

The government of Norway does not accept the Sami claims to land rights. In the meantime, some changes are occurring. In the county of Finnmark, the management of common land has been transferred to a corporation/public company, the *Statsskog*, with the state as the only shareholder. This change has had an impact on land management because it is based on profit making. In other areas farther south land ownership is undergoing further changes, and some Sami are gaining private rights to the land in their local districts. They have asserted their rights and are going to obtain ownership of some areas close to their settlements. A special court is settling the borders between state-owned land and private land. This means that in some areas in Troms and Nordland counties there is now established a propertied class instead of community-owned property. The process of providing private ownership continues, and a commission, the *Høyfjellskomisjonen,* is working to clarify the situation. The President of the *Sámediggi* [Sami Parliament] in Norway, Ole Henrik Magga, has pointed out, however, that "Sami interests are treated in a most unsatisfactory way in this process" (Speech at the 5th Common Property Conference, 1995). On the other hand, the Reindeer Breeders Association in Norway [NRL] is working for the rights of reindeer herding as an industry and not as a part of the Sami Rights legislation. Therefore, processes are going on concerning both ownership and management of Sami land.

It might be thought that Sami people have now achieved their goal of self-government, as they have the *Sámediggi,* the Sami Parliament, with 39 representatives elected by and among the Samis. The area of competence and authority of the Sami Parliament is governed by the Sami Act of June 12th, 1987, which outlines all matters that are, in the opinion of the Norwegian Parliament, of particular concern to the Sami people. The Sami Parliament has a mainly consultative authority. However, Ole Henrik Magga, the president of the *Sámediggi* "recognizes that the Parliament is in the process of becoming an influential body in Sami matters" (Magga 1994).

The *Sámediggi* does not have authority in matters concerning reindeer husbandry or land use. Magga points out, however, that the *Sámediggi* has discussed reindeer herding and fishing at great length, and it has gained influence in both areas. He would like to see more Sami influence in vital Sami issues such as reindeer management, and some veto power in the Norwegian Parliament on issues concerning the management of central Sami resources (Magga, 1994:47).

Some institutional conditions – managing collectively, a model

If there is a willingness to collectively manage the land, there exist both the opportunity to do so and models to follow. In Canada the solution has been to pursue common land management on the local, rather than national, level. This solution is expressed in the model called "Co-management," which, briefly, calls for a body authorized to manage the natural resources in a particular area, i.e. the land, the wildlife and/or the fisheries. Co-management refers to institutional arrangements into which the national level-agencies with jurisdiction over resources enter legally, and where the decision-making is shared. Thus, Co-management is a joint management process that brings together local resource users and government agencies to share the management and responsibility for local or regional resources. (Roberts 1995).

This model, Co-management, has been used in the settlement of land claims made by Canadian aboriginal peoples, who, by the Canadian Constitution Act (1982), are defined as Indian, Inuit, and Metis (Boldt & Long 1985). The first such agreement in Canada, the James Bay and Northern Quebec Agreement (1975), is recognized as a successful one (Diamond 1985:265-285, Pinkerton 1988:17). The second one, the Inuvialuit Agreement (IFA-1984)[5], concerns management of renewable resources without affecting the rights and the obligations of the individuals as Canadian citizens (IFA,1984:4). The basic goals of the Inuvialuit Agreement are:

119

a) to preserve Inuvialuit cultural identity and values within a changing northern society;
b) to enable Inuvialuit to be equal and meaningful participants in the northern and the national economy and society; and
c) to protect and preserve the Arctic wildlife, environment and biological productivity (IFA 1984:2).

The agreement grants control over any type of commercial activity on the lands and water within the region to five committees appointed to manage the renewable resources (item c, above). Each of the committees is made up of equal numbers of Inuvialuit and Canadian Government members. One of the committees is for fishery management; two are for wildlife management in the Northwest Territories and the North Slope, and in Yukon Territory, respectively. There is also an environmental impact assessment committee, and lastly an environmental impact review board (Binder & Hanbidge 1991).

The Inuvialuit members on the committees are appointed by the Inuvialuit Game Council, whose members, in turn, are elected by the Hunters and Trappers Committees (one in each of the six communities of Inuvik, Aklavik, Tuktoyaktuk, Paulatuk, Sachs Harbour and Holman). The Inuvialuit members of the committees are accountable to the Game Council, which represents the collective Inuvialuit interest in renewable resource matters. The Inuvialuit Game Council is a policy-making body, and it interacts with governmental management bodies through the committees.

In addition to the Hunters and Trappers Committee, each community has a Community Corporation, and through these the members of the Inuvialuit Regional Corporation are elected. It is this body's responsibility to conduct and carry out goals other than management of the renewable resources, i.e. goals oriented toward development. My short presentation shows that there are created functional institutions and a corporate structure in connection with the Agreement (IFA 1984:6), and these carry out the decisions made by bodies of the co-management system.

The decision-makers on the national level are often accused of not having sufficient knowledge about the situation on the local level, and there have been discussions between the pastoralists and the biologists on their respective opinions concerning the carrying capacity of certain areas. Due to its focus on the local level and the knowledge of user groups, the co-management system allows the rules to be less detailed, and a more comprehensive decision-making accorded developing communities where the traditional economy based on land and animals is the core and where it is neither possible nor desirable to separate them. When the aim is to maintain a comprehensive development, the co-management regime represents self-governance at a local level and in that manner is a tool to link the land use, cultural preservation, and economic development together.

Conclusion

The land constitutes an economic basis, while land use serves as a core for the culture, and knowledge is maintained through interaction between land use and culture. Knowledge, in turn serves as a technology in maintaining reindeer husbandry; in that sense, the economic development and cultural preservation go together. The interaction between land and technology constitutes the basis of a comprehensive view that protects the environment and allows for controlled use when it comes to harvesting renewable resources. First and foremost, the environmental challenges for the present are connected to limiting the number of animals. At the same time, all the residents in the Sami settlement region have to understand and avoid the unfortunate consequences of the misuse of modern technology.

The President of the *Sámediggi* has, in general terms, complained that knowledge about the Sami people's condition is still greatly lacking in the decision-making bodies, and he asks how the responsibility can be managed well when such basic knowledge about matters at hand is so deficient (Magga 1994:48-49). A co-management system allows knowledge from the local level, including that of the user groups, to enter the decision-making process. The user groups thereby have an opportunity to contribute their knowledge of, for instance, the carrying capacity, distribution of pastures and animals, and traditional use of land, based on Sami customary law etc. Therefore, Sami traditional knowledge should be included in the discourse of resource management. However, it is necessary to do research in order to enhance the application of this knowledge in matters of management.

In order to achieve true development, some institutions and procedures must be established. These have to be in accordance with the prevalent beliefs and values that individuals hold regarding their government process. Therefore, a further step must be taken to design new management arrangements. There is hope in the increasing demands from Sami organizations to become more involved in the management of natural resources. Collective management should be the starting point, and some form of co-management arrangement could be a tool to obtain comprehensive development. Such a solution is especially relevant in Finnmark county and North-Troms, where keeping reindeer is a very important industry. At the same time, the population in this area is heterogenous, and conflicts between the pastoralists and others with vested interest in land use occur. Such a region really needs co-operation, even if the challenges to succeed in managing together are problematic.

Management of the reindeer districts is directed toward the optimum output of meat by means of regulations governing the pastures and the number of animals and herders. In order to attain comprehensive development, some structures must be changed to include power structures which take care of both economic development and culture. However, the pastoralists are but a minority within the Sami people, and they are unconvinced that there will be any advantage in sharing power with non-pastoralists. I therefore point out that laws governing the rights of reindeer industry, such as the Reindeer Herding Act, will, as of now, be amended only by the Norwegian Parliament as a legislative assembly.

Even if there are differences in conditions found in two countries, the Co-management arrangements developed in Canada and based on agreements signed by the government and the local user groups can provide a valuable model for managing the land in the main Sami settlement region.

The Sami Parliament has succeeded in obtaining influence especially on the national level. In order to achieve the goal of managing renewable resources and preserving Sami culture, an efficient body must be designed to maintain land use. Due to unstable relationships and conflicts, initiating changes will be a challenge. Designing and establishing a body or bodies will mean exercising influence in vital Sami issues on the local level. In this matter, Sami Parliament ought to initiate a process of co-operation. This process could start, even if the issue of ownership of the Sami land is un-resolved. However, different participants have different objectives. Therefore, it is a question of who participates, because designing structures is a critical problem and it involves the question who defines and dictates the terms regarding knowledge as an appropriate technology. I repeat that the point will be that user groups should enter the agenda and that they have rights, power, and obligations with respect to management of resources in a particular area.

1   Pastoralism is based on reindeer as the one and only resource. The other main mechanism in reindeer husbandry is based on exploitation of several resources, i.e. that keeping reindeer is combined with handicraft, tourism business, berry-picking etc.(Kalstad 1996).

2   In 1994 and 1996 I was happy to travel abroad thanks to funding from the Research Council of Norway, and therefore my consideration of the model for co-management has empirical support acquired in the Inuvialuit Settlement Region in the Northwest Territories. In this con-nection I want to thank people in Inuvik and Tuktoyaktuk and special

thanks go to the staff at the Inuvialuit Renewable Resources Committees Joint Secretariat. I owe a great deal to the Binders who hosted and ushered my family and me in their ways of life, and we also had experiences of whaling in the Beaufort Sea close to Richard Island.

3   The dual spelling of some Sami place names is due to the principle in the Sami Language Act, which ensures the use of Sami place names in order to make the Sami names more visible in public. Road signs and map references are also given in Sami language in the parts of Sapmi covered by the new law.

4   There are approximately 250,000 reindeer in Sweden and 200,000 animals in Finland (Beach 1990:273).

5   A few years ago the Gwich'in, who live in the neighborhood of the Inuvialuit, also attained their own land rights settlement agreement (Gwich'in Comprehensive Land Claim Agreement 1992).

References:

Beach, Hugh. 1990. "Comparative Systems of Reindeer Herding", Galaty, Jon G. and Johnston, Douglas L.: *The World of Pastoralism*. The Guilford Press, New York: 255-298.

Berkes, Fikret. 1994. "Co-management: Bridging the Two Solitudes", *Northern Perspectives,* Vol. 22. 2-3, Summer/Fall 1994. Canadian Arctic Resources Committee, Ottawa.

Binder, Lloyd N. & Hanbidge, Bruce. 1991. "Aboriginal People and Resource Co-management. The Inuvialuit of the Western Arctic and Resource Co-management under a Land Claims Settlement." *Paper presented at Common Property Conference,* September 26-29, Winnipeg, Canada.

Bjørklund, Ivar. 1990. "Sami Reindeer Pastoralism as an Indigenous Resource Management System in Northern Norway: A Contribution to the Common Property Debate," *Development and Change.* Vol.2: 75-86. SAGE, London, Newbury Park and New Delhi.

Bjørklund, Ivar. 1994. *Diedut No. 1-1994,* The World Commission on Culture and Development. Majority-Minority Relations. The Case of the Sami in Scandinavia, Report, Guovdageaidnu, Norway. July 1993. Sámi Instituhtta.

Boldt, Mienno & Long, J. Anthony, (eds.). 1985. *The Quest for Justice. Aborigi-*

nal Peoples and Aboriginal Rights, University of Toronto Press.

Diamond, Billy. 1985. "Aborigianal Rights. The James Bay Experience" in Boldt, Mienno & Long, J. Anthony, (ed). *The Quest for Justice.* Aboriginal Peoples and Aboriginal Rights, University of Toronto Press: 265-285.

Ingold, Tim.1980. *Hunters, Pastoralist and Ranchers. Reindeer Economies and their Transformations,* Cambridge University Press.

Ingold, Tim. 1986. *The appropriation of nature. Essays on human ecology and social relations,* Manchester University Press.

Jentoft, Svein. 1989. "Fisheries co-management. Delegating government responsibility to fishermen's organizations" in *Marine Policy No. 13:2.*

Jentoft, Svein. 1993. *Danglinglines. The Fisheries Crisis and the Future of Coastal Communities. The Norwegian Experience.* Institute of Social and Economic Research, Memorial University of Newfoundland, St. John's.

Kalstad, Johan Klemet Hætta. 1991. *Boazodoallu Sámis. Planet ruvnnuid ja eallima. Reindrift for inntekt, arbeid og kultur,* Post-graduate thesis, Institute for Social Science, University of Tromsø.

Kalstad, Johan Klemet Hætta. 1994. "Kunnskap om kunnskap. Om reinforskning og dens institusjonelle vilkår", *Bærekraftig forvaltning av biologiske fellesressurser,* The Norwegian National MAB-Committee, The Research Council of Norway.

Kalstad, Johan Klemet Hætta. 1996. "The Modern Challenge Facing Knowledge in Sami Subsistence," *Diedut 1996:4,* Sami Instituhtta. Guovdageaidnu: 21-30.

Kalstad, Johan Klemet Hætta. 1994. "Pastoralism and Management of Common Land in Finnmark," Paper presented at the 5th Common Property Conference of the International Association for the Study of Common Property, Bodø.

Kalstad, Johan Klemet Hætta & Viken, Arvid. 1996. "Sami Tourism - Traditional Knowledge Challenged by Modernity," *Diedut 1996:4,* Sámi Instituhtta. Guovdageaidnu: 31-43.

Magga, Ole Henrik. 1994. *Diedut No. 1-1994.* The World Commission on Culture and Development, Majority-Minority Relations, The Case of the Sami in Scandinavia, Report, July 1993, Sámi Instituhtta, Guovdageidnu.

Magga, Ole Henrik. 1995. "Rights for Indigenous Peoples," Speech at the 5th Common Property Conference, Bodø, Norway May 24-28, 1995.

Ostrom, Elinor. 1992. *Crafting Institutions for Self-Governing Irrigation Systems,*

Institute for Contemporary Studies, San Francisco.

Paine, Robert. 1964. "Herding and Husbandry. Two basic distinctions in the analysis of reindeer management," *Folk 6:1.*

Paine, Robert. 1994. *Herds of the Tundra. A Portrait of Sami Reindeer Pastoralism,* Smithsonian Institution Press, Washington and London.

Pinkerton, Evelyn. (ed.) 1989. *Co-Operative Management of Local Fisheries. New Direction for Improved Management and Community Development,* University of British Columbia Press, Vancouver.

Roberts, Karen. 1995. *Circumpolar Aborigiginal People and Co-mangemnet Practice,* Presented at the Conference of the International Association for the Study of Common Property, Bodø.

The Sami People. 1990. Sámi Instituhtta, Guovdageaidnu. Davvi Girji OS. Kárášjohka.

Vorren, Ørnulf. 1962. *Finnmarkssamenes nomadisme I.* Universitetsforlaget, Oslo.

Reports

NOU 1993:34. *Rett til og forvaltning av land og vann i Finnmark,* Justis- og politidepartementet, Oslo.

Reindriften i Finnmark. Forslag til ny distriktsinndeling i Finnmark, Januar 1994. Reindriftsadminsitrasjonen, Alta.

St.meld.nr. 28 (91-92) *En bærekraftig reindrift.* Landbruksdepartementet. Oslo.

The Inuvialuit Final Agreement (IFA). 1984. Department for Indian and Northern Affairs, Ottawa.

Siv Kvernmo

Developing Sami Health Services – A Medical and Cultural Challenge

The Sami people have inhabited and continue to inhabit large areas of northern Fennoscandia that fall within the borders of several nations. As a result, health services for the Sami have varied and been dependent on the state of national health and resources within each country, even though the Sami, as a minority population, have been in a special situation that transcends national borders. Attention given to the development of a separate health service for the Sami has varied greatly, both within each country and from one nation to the next. Without a doubt, Norway, and particularly the county of Finnmark, has come the farthest in this area. Finnmark is the geographical region in Scandinavia with the highest concentration of Sami and where the Sami language and culture have best survived a strict assimilation policy that was at one time set forth by national authorities. In the course of the last few decades increased attention has been directed towards prioritizing the unique needs of Sami medical patients with regard to language, culture, and ethnicity. An important factor in the development of a customized health service has been the fact that most of the Sami health workers who have been involved in this developmental work have themselves come from the area. These workers have returned to their home districts upon completing their education, and many work actively through the Sami health workers' organizations to improve health services for Sami patients. Nowhere else in Norway or other Nordic countries inhabited by Sami does one find a similar situation. A descrip-

127

tion of the Sami health service is, therefore, best illustrated by a look at the developments that have taken place in the province of Finnmark, Norway.

The Medical history of the Sami

Until the 1600s there were neither doctors nor organized health care in Norway. Treatment of illness was the work of local or traveling healers, whose effectiveness was quite varied. Such treatment most often consisted of traditional folk medicine, prayer, and so-called "shamanism" (Steen 1968).

The Sami had their own healers, called in the Sami language *buorredeaddji*. These were the local practitioners of folk medicine, who used everything from herbs, the internal organs of reindeer, religious recitations and charms, and laying on of hands, to bloodletting. Well known is the reading from the Scriptures to stop haemorrhaging, a method that is in use to this day.

In 1775, Finnmark became the first province in which a district surgery was established, and, in 1778, the first physician was appointed to this office. With a geographical area as large as all of Denmark and a widely diffused population consisting of no more than 5-6,000 people, it is clear that access to medical assistance was limited. Just as before, people in Finnmark had to make do as best they could. Only in the latter half of the 19th century did more doctors come to the province, where each was assigned responsibility for health services within an individual district.

The earliest doctors' responsibilities consisted largely of fighting epidemics. The diseases that claimed many lives, Sami and Norwegian alike, during the 18th and 19th centuries were typhus, diphtheria, and tuberculosis. It cannot be said that these diseases were more prevalent among the Sami than among other segments of the population, although living conditions, hygiene, and nutrition among the Sami are described in several sources as being worse than those of the Norwegians.

The Sami population in several districts and its general state of health and standard of living are described in medical reports submitted by doctors working there between 1869 and 1926. These descriptions and characteristics no doubt reflect, to a large extent, a negative attitude toward the Sami on the part of the doctors, as well as the fact that several of the latter were assigned to work among a people who differed greatly, both linguistically and culturally, from what they considered to be the norm. In a few reports, however, one can find a more varied and even positive view of the Sami, but such reports are the exception.

The coastal Sami, who lived in fjord districts and along the coast, were described as the poorest and most degenerate within the population. The terms "dirty" and "lazy" were often used to describe them; and illnesses that were particularly widespread among the coastal Sami were attributed in some medical reports to the victims' belonging to a degenerate race (Wessel 1918).

On the coast, Sami lived for the most part in earth huts and subsisted on fishing and farming. Earth and sod huts were used as shelter for both people and livestock from the earliest period of settlement in the Sami regions until a few decades ago. These huts were not an inadequate form of housing, rather, they were built according to the need for a snug, sturdy home in a harsh climate where construction materials were very limited. In fact, all it cost the coastal Sami to build such dwellings was his own labor and a relatively small amount of time. Norwegians who had no knowledge of this form of building – such as the Norwegian doctors in the Sami districts – were highly skeptical toward the earth hut and often described it as an unsuitable shelter for human beings.

Inland, reindeer herding was the most common form of livelihood. There, the housing standard was described as being significantly better than that of Sami living on the coast. Sami who led a settled – as opposed to migratory – way of life and were not engaged in reindeer herding most often lived in spacious log houses and based their livelihood on farming and hunting. Those who were

129

herders used both earth huts and *lávvu* – the Sami tent, as dwellings. Sami living inland were also among the first to develop agriculture in Finnmark. Reindeer herders were characterized by several doctors as being the wealthiest and most prominent Sami, but also the most unsanitary.

The Sami's health condition, before and now

Concerning illness, Sami were to some degree plagued by the same diseases in earlier times as were Norwegians living in the same area, although through the years Finnmark, including the core Sami districts, has had a high rate of illness and death. According to medical reports from the end of the 1840s, the Sami population did not suffer from scurvy, as did the Norwegians and Kvens (Finnish settlers in Norway). This can be explained by the fact that the Sami diet was different from that of the Norwegians. Sami had traditionally included in their diet plants and vegetation, such as sorrel, which contain a lot of vitamin C. The same nutritional function was served by reindeer milk mixed with crowberries and frozen in clean reindeer stomachs in the fall. During the course of the winter, slices were cut from this frozen mixture of milk and vitamin C-rich fruit, which were then thawed before being consumed.

Gradually, however, the Sami diet changed. Ancient traditions were set aside and forgotten in favor of foods that had become available through increased contact with Norwegian society. A great deal of coffee and sugar were consumed. Breast milk for small children, who had often continued to be nursed until they were two years old, was frequently replaced with a mixture of milk and coffee, a beverage not particularly suited to growing children.

To this day, the rate of infant mortality has been highest in Finnmark. Families were large, and it was expected that one or more children would die before reaching adulthood. There were few trained midwives, and every rural community relied on the help of a woman who had herself recently given birth and could lend a hand at childbirth.

Congenital hip dislocation was a common problem, which many attributed to infants' being wrapped in swaddling clothes and kept in portable Sami cradles. This is not a feasible argument, however, since hip dislocation was no more prevalent among reindeer herders, who used this form of cradle to the greatest extent, than among other Sami. Heredity was another explanation set forth, along with the theory that the Sami are a degenerate race. Today, however, one certainly prefers to blame lack of proper diagnosis and treatment, rather than a higher incidence of the disease, for the presence of this condition.

Few systematic investigations of illness among the Sami have been conducted within recent years. Isolated studies, such as those of coronary disease in Finnmark, have shown a lower incidence among Sami than among Norwegians and Finns. That increase which one nonetheless finds in the number of cases today can be seen in connection with the changes in eating habits and lifestyle that Sami have undergone as a result of their increased contact with the dominant society.

Milk sugar intolerance has been found to occur relatively frequently among the Sami. According to Finnish researchers, over 30% of the Sami population in Finland suffers from this intolerance. For the sake of comparison, it can be said that only 6% of the Norwegian population suffers from this disease (Sahi 1980).

As stated above, hip joint disorders have been assumed to occur more often among Sami than among, for example, Norwegians. More recent research shows that approximately 30% of the Sami population suffers from this affliction. Bechterev's disease (ankylosing spondylitis) has also demonstrated a greater frequency in this group (1.8 %) compared with Norwegians (.6 %) (Johnsen 1992). Only a few North American Indian tribes have a higher incidence of this illness than do the Sami.

There have been no investigations of psychosomatic illnesses in the Sami districts. What physicians and other health professionals are left with is the clinical experience that this is a frequent problem of the kind that is found among other minority groups in other countries. Among psychological disorders, depression and melancholy are shown to be the most prevalent among women and men living in the Sami population centers (Brevik, Dahlgard, and Fylkesnes 1993).

The Sami situation in the Norwegian health-care system

An investigation of the health-care situation in a little Sami community in a fjord area showed that Sami visited the doctor far less often than did Norwegians (Fuggelli 1986). They had more hidden illnesses than others and received inadequate follow-up on diagnosed illnesses in more cases than did Norwegians. Accordingly, nine out of ten instances of illness were either neglected or covered up. An investigation from 1987 of Sami patients operated on for appendicitis at a hospital in Finnmark showed that Sami-speaking patients remained hospitalized nearly twice as long after their operations as did those who spoke Norwegian. Furthermore, 25% more blood tests were performed on Sami-speaking patients, who were also operated on more hastily than were Norwegian-speaking patients and suffered more post-surgical complications and more false cases of appendicitis. Although this investigation included relatively few patients, it gives us a view of a Norwegian health care system that tries to compensate for a communication problem with a greater number of examinations and prolonged hospital stays without improved results. This study and the experiences of both Sami patients and health care staff point to the fact that a language problem does exist, not only among the Sami-speaking patients, but also among the Norwegian medical practitioners – a language problem which can, in fact, lead to serious consequences for the relationship between the Norwegian health care system and Sami patients.

Health services to the Sami

In addition to the official health services, Sami have availed themselves of their own healers, who have been accepted by the people right up to this day and seen as a relevant source of treatment, alongside formal medical expertise. A parallel can be drawn here with the western world's current search for alternative forms of treatment to supplement today's medical science. Moreover, the Sami healers, with their insider status and understanding of Sami language and culture gain the trust and confidence of their Sami patients.

Following WW II, a full-fledged health service was developed in Norway. Meanwhile, the shortage of doctors in Finnmark was and has continued to be greater than anywhere else in the nation. The standard of health in Finnmark has always been the worst in Norway. The lack of doctors has meant that both prophylactic and curative treatment has remained at a low level. After WW II the long-standing policy of assimilation was replaced by a planned integration of Sami society into the Norwegian nation state. The Sami were to become equal members of the state, not as a separate group, but as individual members with equal rights as Norwegians. At this time the Sami were not considered to need a culturally and linguistically adapted health care system. At this time, any special health services for the Sami in their own language would have been contrary to the general plan. As early as the nineteenth century, doctors who worked in the Sami districts described the communication problems that arose during their consultations with Sami patients, namely, the great difficulty on the part of patients to explain themselves in a foreign language – Norwegian – and on the part of health workers to give both information and correct treatment in another language – Sami – that was foreign to them.

In several areas, the Sami's standard of living was lower than that of Norwegians. A movement for better housing was therefore begun in the Sami municipalities during the 1960s. Still, if others considered their standard of living to be low, the Sami themselves didn´t necessarily always agree, since concepts of what constitutes a good life and good health are culturally determined.

In 1957, the Sami Commission presented its recommendations. It especially addressed the state of Sami health and housing. On the basis of a report from the chief medical officer for Finnmark, it suggested that several measures be taken (Jonassen 1959). At the time, there was not a single trained Sami physician and very few Sami in other health professions. The Sami Commission recommended special admission quotas for Sami students applying to medical schools. It also requested an increase in the number of trained Sami nurses and public health nurses and the establishment of positions for public health nurses who would carry out health education in Sami-speaking districts.

Why a special Sami health service?

The importance of language:

As early as the 19th century, Norwegian doctors working in the Sami areas complained about the problems imposed by language during their contact with Sami patients and about the implications this could have for treatment (Forsdahl 1990). The language problem was defined as being that of the Sami, not of the Norwegian doctors. To a certain extent, Sami patients have for some time had the right to be provided with an interpreter, but this service has been occasional and poorly organized. Most often, Sami patients have brought along relatives to act as personal interpreters. Those who were engaged as interpreters were most often laymen, who, as a rule, had few qualifications for the job. Should an occasion arise at a hospital, for example, where a person who speaks Sami was needed to interpret, another patient might be called upon, without regard for questions of confidentiality or professionality. Several investigations show that Sami-speaking patients – and reindeer herders, in particular – experience difficulty communicating with Norwegian-speaking doctors (Brekke 1983, Sandvik 1988). A consumer survey regarding doctors' services in the Sami municipality, Kautokeino, shows that there was a relatively greater insufficiency of information provided by doctors to Sami patients than to Norwegian patients. Approximately 60% of the Sami-, but none of the Norwegian-speaking patients had difficulty understanding the physicians. 23% of those speaking Sami desired that an interpreter be present during the consultation without there being one made available (Sandvik 1988). In Fuggelli's investigation, conducted in a small Sami community in 1980, 65% of the patients admitted that language difficulties prevented them from seeking a physician (Fuggelli 1986).

A Sami patient's language ability will vary according to his or her age and geographical location. Today, it is the elderly and children in the core Sami districts who are bilingual to the least degree and least able to avail themselves of information and treatment in the Norwegian language. Although many Sami are able to speak relatively good Norwegian, they still feel that communication with the health worker is easier in Sami. Today, it is mainly in the core Sami districts that Sami patients are able to use their own language, except in the hospital setting, where this is only occasionally the case. An interpreter service has been established at some hospitals, but only in the last few years.

Cultural understanding:

In addition to linguistic differences, cultural differences between practitioners and Sami patients also enter the picture. It has been assumed that the understanding of illness and the tradition of treatment are for the Sami what they are for the rest of the population. What has been lacking is the placing of symptoms and disease into a cultural context. An example is the concept of pain. Several physicians report that Sami patients often express their emotional problems physically, in terms of pain, that is, they describe their problems psychosomatically. This may be connected to the fact that the Sami language has few words for feelings.

To offer a service where the individual feels comfortable, both culturally and linguistically, is to grant greater and fairer accessibility to those who need it. Striving for this goal is a long-term process. Within child and adolescent psychiatry, emphasis has been placed on training practitioners in cross-cultural understanding. An important professional resource person in this work has been a social anthropologist who is associated with the clinic at Karasjok. Transcultural education has drawn professionals from various areas of health and social services in Finnmark. The training program was at one time established with Norwegian caregivers in mind, since Sami practitioners were assumed to already have the necessary knowledge and skills. Gradually, however, it has been more and more recognized that Sami practitioners, too, require an analytical approach to their own ethnicity and culture.

This recognition has now expanded to several levels within the health and social services. The Sami Medical Association has worked to introduce ethnic medicine as a separate subject in medical education. This is now an integral part of the curriculum for both the medical school and several other programs at the University of Tromsø. Cross-cultural pedagogy is offered at the Sami College in Kautokeino.

Education and recruitment of Sami-speaking health care workers

The Sami Commission's recommendation regarding education of Sami doctors was set in motion in 1963. Its justification was that, because of language difficulties, Sami-speaking students could not compete effectively for the limited number of openings within certain fields of study. At the same time, there was a need for Sami-speaking doctors. Two openings, with reduced entrance requirements, were set allocated for Sami-speaking students at the University of Bergen´s School of Medicine, a controversial and debated arrangement. Still, the special quota system at the School of Medicine at Bergen has been extremely important for the training of Sami physicians. Approximately 13 Sami physicians have been trained by means of this arrangement since it was introduced. The first graduated in 1970.

Since its establishment in 1973, the University of Tromsø Medical School has graduated several Sami doctors. Here, too, there are openings earmarked for Sami students, and it appears that it is easier for Sami students to receive their education in their own part of the country than in another, since more and more are applying for entrance to the School of Medicine at Tromsø, while the openings at Bergen are seldom filled. Today, there are approximately 30 fully-trained Sami physicians and approximately 12 Sami medical students in Norway out of a population of about 30,000 Sami.

The number of Sami has increased within other health professions as well, thanks to the quota system and extra credit given for language competency. For its size, the Sami community today has a considerable number of social workers and other health-care workers, and yet shortages still exist in several areas. For example, there continue to be few or no Sami-speaking psychologists, pharmacists, or odontologists.

A great many Sami young people who have completed their education have returned to the Sami regions. The strategy of training Sami young people and encouraging them to return to Sami-speaking areas upon completion of their studies has worked well.

Sami health organizations

In 1984, Sami doctors organized themselves into the Sami Medical Association (Samisk Legeforening). The object of the association has been to work for improved health services for the Sami people and an adaptation of these services, both linguistically and culturally. Further, it has worked to promote health education among the Sami and to encourage both the education of Sami doctors and training in ethnic medicine within various health professions. In the mid-1980s Sami nurses and social workers also organized their own associations. These three organizations have played an important role in the development of a Sami health and social service that began to gather momentum during the 1980s. They have been driving forces in the effort to inform others of Sami patients' needs and the importance of training Sami health professionals, establishing special health services, and so on. In 1986, the first conference to discuss policies for Sami health services was held. Among its participants were national and provincial officials and other interested parties. This meeting threw light for the first time on Sami patients' particular situation within the Norwegian health care system, and it became an important step toward the continuation of work for a Sami health service.

Special health services for the Sami

Today, there are several health institutions in the key Sami region whose particular assignment it is to offer to the Sami people services that include psychiatry, alcohol counseling and treatment, child services, family services, as well as such physical health services as rheumatology, internal medicine, cardiology, and ear-nose-and-throat. In addition, primary health care is available in the various Sami municipalities. Health care on the specialist level is based on two different models: the somatic (i.e. physical) health services are private, while all others are managed by the provincial government of Finnmark. Both private practices and public services receive economic support from the Norwegian government.

The first Sami medical students were already discussing in the 1960s the idea of offering, in the Sami language, the services of specialists in a number of fields of medicine. This idea took on immediate importance when the first Sami medical specialists had completed their training. Supported by Sami health organizations and by some individuals, the struggle was begun to establish a separate center for specialized medicine within the core Sami areas in Finnmark. This objective encountered a great deal of opposition from provincial authorities as well as from colleagues in hospitals, since the idea of polyclinical services being offered outside the hospital setting was extremely uncommon. The province of Finnmark lacked a number of medical specialists at its hospitals, and it was hoped that Sami specialists would fill these positions. Meanwhile, the Sami physicians maintained that they wished to provide services in the Sami language in a Sami district, where patients might feel comfortable, both culturally and linguistically. This argument was little understood, and no funds were appropriated by the province to support it. The national government, on the other hand, responded favorably to the idea and granted special funds for health services to the Sami population.

Today, there are three Sami-speaking medical specialists within somatic health services for the Sami, and their presence is very much appreciated by both Sami and Norwegian inhabitants of the area.

When it comes to Sami-speaking practitioners, the situation is best in somatic health services, that is, in secondary, specialized medical care. Here, all physicians and all support staff speak Sami. The situation in psychiatry and family and alcohol counseling is not quite so good. Services in neither adult nor child and adolescent psychiatry are provided by Sami-speaking physicians or psychologists. One Sami-speaking person is currently receiving training in child and adolescent psychology.

139

When it comes to primary care, only occasionally are patients able to have consultations with a general practitioner in the Sami language. In some of the Sami communities there are, at this writing, one or two Sami-speaking doctors. Things are quite different in the areas of nursing care and social work . Today there are many Sami-speaking nurses and social workers who have returned to their home communities after completing their education. The goal is that, in the future, Sami patients will have the opportunity to use their own language when receiving care within the health service. The means to attain this goal lie in motivating more Sami-speaking young people to attain a higher education.

Challenges for the future of Sami health care

Sami health care is a new concept. As health professionals, we face many demanding challenges. We must design a health care service that is based on the Sami people´s needs, way of thinking, and traditions. This can mean that health care in the Sami districts has to be given another form than that found in the majority society. This could come into conflict with the view that we, as professionals, have gained through training and our respective professions, as well as with those rules and norms that apply to health service as it exists in Norway today. The cross-cultural perspective must be incorporated, not only by Sami professionals, but equally as much by politicians, our Norwegian colleagues, and public officials. Cooperation with those in other professions, such as social scientists, anthropologists, linguists, and sociologists is important if the development of an ethnically and culturally adapted health service is to succeed. This work is still in its infancy.

Experience thus far has shown that it is important to build up a central, formative base for Sami health services. Today, we have few Sami-speaking professionals and a great need for services offered in the Sami language. In order to give Sami professionals opportunities for professional growth and stimulation, collegial cooperation, and opportunities for systematization of experiences, *we will for some time have to centralize access to services offered in the Sami language by specialists.* This will mean that the services which today are offered in Karasjok in Finnmark must be preserved and given the possibility for further expansion. In addition, this center offering various services must be organized in such a way that each health institution will not exist in isolation, with few professional staff members and little contact with other institutions. The desire for quality is of importance within the Sami health services, as well. Better organization will also yield possibilities to utilize human resources more effectively. These will be important initial strategies. The next phase must be the exportation of our competence to other Sami regions and, eventually, to Norwegian society.

References:

Brevik, J.I., et al. 1993. "Psykisk helse i Finnmark. Gode levekår som helsefremmende strategi?," Pedersen, N.P. (ed), *Fylkeslegens skrifterie,* No. 1: 55-58.

Forsdahl, A. 1991. "Utdrag av medisinalberetninger fra Finnmark 1863 - 1929," *Fylkeslegen i Finnmarks skriftserie,* No. 5.

Fuggeli, P. 1986. "Skjult helsebehov blant samer?," *Sami medica* 3: 43-53.

Hansen, M. and Hansen, H.A. 1983. Resultater fra en praksisregistrering i Karasjok, Nov.

Johannesen, A. 1987. En undersøkelse av samisk- og norsktalende innlagt på Hammerfest sykehus med diagnosen akutt abdomen. Valgfri oppgave i st. IV, Medisinerstudiet, Fagområdet medisin, Universitetet i Tromsø.

Johnsen, K., et al. 1992. "The prevalence of ankylosing spondylitis among Norwegian Samis (Lapps)," *The Journal of Rheumatology* 19(10):1591-1594.

Jonassen, Ø. 1959. "Sosiale og hygieniske forhold i flyttsamenes basisområde," *Tidsskrift for Den Norske Lægeforening* 3:83-89.

Sahi, T. 1994. "Genetics and epidemiology of adult-type hypolactasia," *Scandinavian Journal of Gastroenterology – Supplement,* 202:7-20.

Sandvik, J. 1988. Legetjenesten i Kautokeino kommune – en brukerundersøkelse. Valgfri oppgave i st. IV, Medisinerstudiet, Fagområdet medisin, Universitetet i Tromsø.

Steen, A. 1961. *Samenes folkemedisin,* Oslo & Bergen, Universitetsforlaget.

Wessel, A.B. 1918. "Laaghalte slekter i Finnmarken," *Tidsskrift for Den Norske Lægeforening* 8:337-368.

Vigdis Stordahl

Sami Generations

Sami society in Norway today can be seen as highly differentiated on a generational basis, reflected in a Sami youth culture that is separate and relatively isolated. Sami youth in general insist on their own social space and their own categories of meaning. They strongly argue that adults should have no say in their affairs. The struggle for "places of their own," such as youth houses, engineering workshops, rock clubs etc. is an expression of this urge. To many adults their perception of their children's rejection of them is both provocative and frightening, and underscores issues of parental authority. Many Sami parents also feel that their youngsters risk losing contact with Sami culture because, in their view, Sami culture is not represented in the social space the youth create for themselves. Some even argue that youth clubs and youth houses in reality are institutions of Norwegianization on a par with kindergartens and schools because they include no Sami activities such as *duodji* – Sami handicrafts, and *yoik* – a traditional form of Sami music.

But do today's Sami youth reject their ethnic identity when they do not show the same interest in Sami handicraft and folk music as their parents? Not necessarily! Sami youth of today are concerned with the fact that they are Sami and that Sami culture should survive. When they insist on their own social space and categories of meaning, it is not necessarily Sami culture or their Sami identity they reject but their parents' generation's way of expressing this identity. Let us therefore take a closer look at what it is that has characterized today's parent generation. My material is collected during fieldwork in a large and socially differentiated Sami community in the Sami heartland in inner Finnmark in northern Norway. However, I do think that we also can find these processes in other Sami communities in Norway, and I have therefore taken the liberty to generalize.

Today's parent generation:
"Express your Sami-ness openly"

Today's parent generation were young adults in the 1970s, a decade in which the debate on Sami ethno-political consciousness and cultural revitalization peaked. The 70s was the period in which everything that had been taken from the Sami people was to be returned. The Sami were again to command their own destiny. The century-long policy of assimilation therefore came to an end and a new minority policy and political structure had to be established. The Sami were now to be accepted as a people equal to the Norwegians. This meant, among other things, that the Sami language had to be accepted as an official language and that the Sami were to get control over the resources in their own territories. The latter principle was formulated as "Sami rights to land and water." The overall goal for the new Sami political movement was a better society for the Sami to live in. This society was called *Sápmi,* the territory considered to be traditionally Sami. A Sami artist visualized Sapmi on a map without any national borders crosscutting the territory and with only Sami names on it.

The 1970s saw a political and cultural revitalization never witnessed before in Sami history. Alongside organizational work and the creation of institutions, resolutions were sent to governments, demonstrations and hungers strikes implemented, and national and international seminars and conferences, both political and professional, were arranged. Additionally, new cultural activities now came into being: song and *yoik* festivals; a new Sami literature; and Sami popular music. It was during this period that the ČSV[1] came into being. ČSV became, like "Black Power," "Red Power" and

144

"Women's Power," a concept and a symbol for those who wanted to change the position of the oppressed as well as a label for identifying those who actively joined and supported the Sami political movement. They were "ČSVs." The ČSVs were recognizable, not only because of their strong and revolutionary opinions, but also by virtue of their style of dress. Even though they did not wear the Sami dress daily, they always wore some cultural emblems that signalled that they were Sami: Sami boots, pewter embroidered watch straps, ČSV pins and buttons, sweaters and caps with Sami colors and patterns. Their use of Sami handicraft and folk music was also part of this cultural repertoire.

For the youth of the 1970s, today's parent generation, the life project was to create a Sami identity solely based on Sami traditions such as Sami language, Sami food, Sami costumes, Sami architecture, Sami music, and Sami folktales. This was a life project in opposition to mainstream society. At the same time it was in opposition to their own parents' generation whose life project had been either to keep quiet, hide their Sami identity, or to strive to be as clever as possible in Norwegian language and culture. Everything was done in order to be acceptable as decent people and thus be qualified to take part in Norwegian society. Many feared being sanctioned if they raised their voices against the government or Norwegian authorities. More than hundred year of assimilation policy, the so-called Norweginization (Eriksen & Niemi 1981), had made it's impression in people. To many of this generation the Norwegian welfare state as built up after WW II was a good society to live in. It was a society with a health and social security program, free schooling, new job opportunities and a policy of equal opportunity for every citizen regardless of gender or socio-economic background. The older generation and those in opposition to the Sami Movement were not willing to trade all this away to fight for the Sami to gain a complementary position in Norwegian society. This debate between the young adults joining the Sami Movement and their parents can however, not be fully understood in term of a generational debate. What we witnessed in the 1970s was a "symbolic warfare" (Cohen 1985) being launched against everything Norwegian. Symbolic because the weapons used were signs, symbols and categorizations loaded with ethnic meaning – what Eidheim (1971) calls idioms. A recodification of Sami culture took place. The image of the Sami language was transformed from that of a "dying" language to a "mothertongue"; Sami dress changed from being a marker of a stigmatized ethnic group to a "national dress"; yoik was no longer associated with drunkenness or non-Christian behavior but was seen as "Sami folk music." In other words, idioms were transformed from one context to another and given new meaning in the context of a newly emerging Sami identity (Grønhaug 1974).

In order to mobilize as many as possible to political action, however, the idioms employed have to be symbolically simple. The risk is then that individuals find the idioms too narrow to organize their personal experiences around. How individuals manage their ethnic identity is colored by and refracted through all the complexities in their personal lives and experiences (Cohen 1985). What then happens is that individuals either reject or start disputing the idioms being introduced. In the Sami case we have seen both happen. Under specific local circumstances we can see how even small details in everyday life are turned into big issues of ethnic identity management (cf. Stordahl 1991, 1994, 1996). Thus, processes of ethnic incorporation, or identity politics as it also is termed, is potentially full of dispute and conflicts with consequences not only for the relation between the two ethnic groups involved, but also for the relation between individuals within the group. Thus, the conflicts have not only accelerated between the Norwegian and the Sami society, but also among the Sami. The Sami Movement's construction of a Sami identity for ethnopolitical purposes has been highly debated and even caused conflicts among former friends and families as well as occupational groups, regions and generations.

In retrospect we can see that this symbolic warfare of the Sami Movement was successful. Many of the things which were provocative in the 1970s are today mostly conventional, being accepted by Sami as well as Norwegians. Not only do people talk as a matter of course about Sami art, handicraft, clothes, patterns, colors etc., these former radical idioms have now become consumer commodities in inter-cultural space.

The youth of the 1970s, the former ČSVs or Sami activists, constitute the parent generation of today, and again we are witnessing a generational dispute as to what constitutes Sami identity. However, the dispute is not as pronounced as previously and it is not the existence of a specific Sami identity or the right to be taught Sami language in school or speak it wherever you choose without the risk of being seen as anti-Norwegian that is at stake, as was the case with the former generations. The context, or the frame of reference for today's debate is different – at least for the youth of the 90s.

Today's youth: "It is great to be a Sami, but you don't have to overdo it"

The youth of the 1990s, many of whom are children of the Sami activists, are in a different situation than were their parents two decades ago. The 90s generation is the first generation of Sami, at least in the Sami heartland, to have received training in Sami language and culture throughout their school years. There is reason to believe that this training, together with the intensified debate on Sami issues, has influenced the development of a much more obvious self-image in this generation who, in contrast to their parents, have no lost Sami past to avenge or mourn. This is confirmed in the report of the conversations between Sami children and youth and the Sami consultant for the *Ombudet for barn og unge* (Ombudsman for Children and Youth) (Rapport fra barneombudet 1995).

It was important to the Sami activists of the 70s to make their ethnic identity visible to the public by using various ethnic markers such as Sami clothes or jewelry. This repertoire of signs and symbols no longer has the same meaning in Sami society. They are not charged with the same political meaning as they once were but have, to a great extent, become consumer goods – "Sami handicrafts" – that anyone can buy. To some of the youth this repertoire belongs to a style they do not share. This style belongs to another generation – that of their parents. Others reject these symbols and signs in order to signal an opposition, be it on an individual basis towards their activist parents or other adults, or on a more structural level towards the Sami establishment, the "Super-Samis" as some youth call them. That the Sami activists of the 1970s now have become the Sami establishment is a fact many of them do not face easily. When today's youth reject the symbols of the ČSV period, therefore, it is not Sami culture nor their ethnic identity they reject. They are, on the contrary, claiming their right to determine their own terms and symbols of Sami-ness which they feel appropriate to the demands of their own time. Obvious signs which mark ethnic identity are not seen as significant in this context.

It is understandable that the parent generation of today still is concerned about Sami cultural survival. Participation in the Sami Movement was for them an experience through which their life acquired meaning. In the symbolic warfare launched against everything Norwegian, Sami language and culture were given a positive status and promoted a new sense of Sami self esteem after years of discrimination and feelings of inadequacy and inferiority. It is therefore understandable that the rejection of the symbols of the 1970s is felt as a rejection of Sami heritage and identity. However, many of the ČSV generation have difficulties realizing that their way of demonstrating ethnic identity, their desire to be Sami activists and to behave quite provocatively against other Samis as well as Norwegians, was typical of the spirit of the time. It was the way of expressing ethnic identity typical of the "awakening time."

By not admitting this, they loose sight of the goal they once set – a new and more equal society for the Sami to live in – in many ways has become a reality today. The most recent achievements in this respect have been an amendment to the Norwegian Constitution making it the responsibility of the State to ensure the maintenance of Sami culture; the creation of a Sami Parliament *(Sámediggi)*; and a Sami Language Act which puts Norwegian and Sami on equal footing in specific municipalities. Be this as it may, the modern world and modern life styles make themselves strongly felt also in Sami communities. There are lifestyle demands which do not necessarily coincide with Sami values and norms, and which the ČSV generation tends to classify as Norwegianization in a new guise. For the ČSV in the 1970s the external world posed a threat, at least ideologically. The paradox, however, is the fact that this generation, more than any previous generation, utilizes the opportunities and the modern conveniences the external world has to offer to a full extent. Who else, after all, are more skilled in and familiar with this external world than the ČSVs? They attend international conferences, meet with representatives of the Government and visit holiday resorts abroad.

Ideology aside, we see that one of the reasons why this generation was so successful in its project is the fact that they were skilled in the inter-cultural space of the modern world. They adopted symbols and orientations that fit with their main project – the revitalization of Sami culture. They have become permanent users of modern means of communication like newspapers, TV, radio, music, art and literature, which have had a very positive effect on both Samis and Norwegians in putting Sami culture on a par with Norwegian in the public view. This ability to combine the external and internal world was the strength of the Sami movement in the 1970s. So why then do the former activists tend to react negatively and moralize when the youth of today does the same? Is it possible that they have forgotten that they themselves once were young and oppositional, i.e. that we here are witnessing a typical generational phenomenon?

The challenge to the former activists, who today often belong to the parent generation and to the establishment, is to catch sight of today's youths. In doing so they may discover what challenges contemporary Sami society poses.

Today's Sami challenge

The general development in Norway after WW II has resulted in Sami integration into the Norwegian welfare state and into a much more differentiated and complex Sami society than ever before. Fewer and fewer Sami make a living in primary industry, and more and more make their living as wage earners: teachers, health and social workers, administrators – that is, in occupations which require professional training. Sami politicians seize every opportunity to highlight the demand for Sami with professional training. They urge the youth to return to Sami areas after receiving their educations to fill professional positions.

Education is also seen as the primary means to meet the crisis in the reindeer industry in inner Finnmark. This crisis is a result of overgrazing, and a program has been initiated to effect a better balance between grazing land and herds. The plan is to reduce both the size of the herds and numbers of herd units, and thereby the number of herders. In practice this means that people have to leave reindeer herding or not enter it at all. Part of this program is therefore aimed at persuading more youngsters to go into higher education rather than entering into reindeer herding. For those who either lack the skills or an interest in higher education, the future seems gloomy. They cannot, like their fathers and mothers, choose a livelihood that does not require professional training. For these young people all the talk about education reminds them of their own failure. They feel there is no place and no need for them.

In "the good old days" as today, there were differences among people. Some were richer than others, some belonged to more re-

150

spected families and some came from grander places within the region than others. These social differentiating mechanism are no longer equally important for individual success. Today personal success and social status is based on education. In contemporary Sami society education is not only necessary in order to get a decent job, it is also important in giving individuals the bi-cultural life skills needed to develop the confidence to live and identify oneself as Sami in the modern world.

Traditionally, the dominant view among the Sami has been one in which Norwegian cultural competence has been seen as superior to competence in Sami language and culture which was seen to be of little use in creating a Sami future. The Sami Movement strongly opposed this view, and emphasized that Norwegian and Sami cultural competencies had to be equal in status. In local debates however, these two sets of cultural competencies were looked upon as mutually exclusive. In the late 1960s, when Sami language was first introduced into school curricula, many parents feared that their children would not learn Norwegian properly since it would not be introduced until the third grade. They thus chose only Norwegian language classes for their children. Observing everyday life in Sapmi today, however, we understand that the question is not one of "either - or."

That the decisive factor for success is the combination of Sami and Norwegian cultural competencies appears clear when we consider who currently sets the terms of the ethno-political agenda and who occupies the important positions in Sami society. The positions are mainly held by people who have been active in the Sami political movement. They acquired their skills, be it knowledge of Sami history, language skills or access to the Sami political network by participating in that movement. On the other hand, by participating in politics and in the Norwegian educational system they acquired a Norwegian cultural competence, such as a knowledge of laws, skills to formulate a letter of protest, to write applications, to call at the ministries, to acquire financial support etc. Thus, the success of this ČSV generation to a large extent is due to their success in combining the two sets of cultural competencies, education on the one hand, and Sami identity on the other.

Thus, education is the key to the "good life," be it in the Norwegian or the Sami society. Education provides access to economic and material security as well as providing the more symbolic value of social status. To the Sami population, education has been the key to winning back their history, culture and language. It has been the tool to new knowledge about the Sami as well as to Norwegian culture and society. The danger entailed in education and the change in occupational structure that goes with it is that it tends to marginalize traditional knowledge. Only part of Sami traditional or empirically-based knowledge can be incorporated into a formal educational system because this is a system outside the control of the Sami and ruled by national and international standards. The development of models where knowledge from both Sami and non-Sami systems of knowledge are combined and practiced poses a big challenge to Sami research and educational institutions.

In order to get an education young people usually have to move out of the Sami area. Leaving the safe and known environment for the unknown is not easy for anyone. Young people fear that they will be subject to discrimination because they are Sami, even though few have any personal experience of ethnic discrimination. It is thus important to create a social environment in connection with the colleges and universities attended by Sami students and thus strengthen their self-confidence. The drop-out rate among Sami students is too high. A task of high priority for the ČSV generation should thus be to assume the role of mentors to Sami youth who attend universities.

Gender has also acquired increased significance in contemporary Sami society particularly with reference to the choices young people make when entering adulthood. Approximately 70% of the students at the Sami high school in Karasjok and the Sami teacher training college in Kautokeino are females. There is reason to believe that the process of modernization in contemporary Sami society has given the girls greater confidence than boys when it

152

comes to acquiring the competence needed to get a skilled job. The challenge consists in creating comparable confidence among boys.

The youth think they ought to have a say

In talking with today's youth on issues such as ethnic identity, gender relations and life careers it is clear that they want to maintain Sami culture and heritage. Just as their parents some decades ago, however, they want to have a say in how this heritage is to be managed. If the ČSV generation insists that only their symbols of Sami identity are the correct ones, we should not be surprised if the youth deliberately reject these or invest them with new meaning in order to demonstrate their independence. That the former Sami activists have gone from a position of oppositionality to become what now constitutes the powerful establishment in Sami society seems to be an issue no one really wants to address. Still, many of the youth see this and can report how they, for instance, as youth representatives in Sami organizations have a feeling that they never quite reach the inner circles of Sami politics. Actually, today's youth is in a position in which no previous generation has found itself. They can direct their opposition in two directions: towards the Norwegian system as the Sami activists did, or towards these former activists, who now constitute a new establishment, and there is no risk that today's youth are not aware of their responsibility with respect to their cultural heritage.

1   ČSV is a conbination of frequently used letters in the Sami language. The abbreviation may contain many meanings, e.g., *Čájet Sámi Vuoiŋŋa!* Celebrate Sami Spirit! ČSV came to represent the positiveness of being a Sami.

References:

Cohen, Anthony P. 1985. *The Symbolic Construction of Community,* London, Ellis Horwood Ltd. & Tavistock Publication Ltd.

Eidheim, Harald. 1971. *Aspects of the Lappish Minority Situation,* Oslo, Universitetsforlaget.

Eriksen, Knut Einar & Niemi, Einar. 1981. *Den finske fare,* Oslo, Universitetsforlaget.

Grønhaug, Reidar. 1974. "Transaction and Signification:an analytical distinction in the study of social interaction," Mimeographed, Universitetet i Bergen.

Hovland; Arild. 1996. *Moderne urfolk,* Oslo, Cappelen Akademiske Forlag.

Rapport fra barneombudet: Samiske barn og unge 1995. Ombudet for barn og unge. Oslo.

Stordahl, Vigdis. 1991. "Ethnic integration and identity management – discourses of Sami self-awareness," *North Atlantic Studies* Vol. 3. No. 1.

Stordahl, Vigdis. 1994. "Identity and Saminess: Expressing World View and Nation," *Diedut* No. 1

Stordahl, Vigdis. 1996. *Same i den moderne verden,* Karasjok, Davvi Girji OS.

Jan Henry Keskitalo

Sami Post-Secondary Education

Ideals and Realities

Introduction

In an article in *Journal of American Indian Education* (Barnhardt & Kirkness 1990) the authors focus on the under representation of American Indian/First Nations/Native people in the ranks of college and university graduates in Canada and in the United States. The authors suggest that instead of focusing on the problem as low achievement and placing the onus for adjustment on the student one should focus on how the higher education system functions; the system should respect the students for who they are, showing relevance to their view of the world, and offer reciprocity in their relationship with others and help them exercise responsibility over their own lives. This includes, from what I understand, both individual as well as institutional level challenges.

Eber Hampton (1988) has tried to identify qualities important to an "Indian theory of education," and ends up with a list of standards by which to judge efforts to reach these qualities. Barnhardt & Kirkness (1990) list these as part of the concept of relevance. I find both efforts interesting and worthy when considering ideals and realities in Sami post-secondary education. Now, one could tie these perspectives to the present situation in Sami post-secondary education and try to figure out what elements constitute ideals, and what the realities are. I aim to identify political ideals concerning Sami post-secondary education, further I aim to give some examples of institutional priorities. I will try to compare both with those initially mentioned perspectives, qualities and standards.

The concept of Sami post-secondary education

In a general sense post-secondary education is understood as education delivered through universities and other institutions of higher education, e.g. colleges for semi-professional training, such as colleges of education, regional colleges, colleges of nursing, and colleges of engineering. The concept covers training and certification in research, in professions, as well as in semi-professions or training for certain positions or jobs in society. The post-secondary education sector in Norway covers courses of different length, but the certification levels for semi-professions are at least two years of full-time studies, and the programs cover up to six years of full-time professional training, as well as post-graduate master and doctoral programs. As for individual Sami, the whole range of training at the post-secondary level is available, in principle, since they are Norwegian citizens. But, the programs, in general, are based on the nationwide concept of professional training, with no emphasis on explicit training for a Sami society. This can be understood as the nationwide mainstream of education. Recruiting to jobs in a Sami society from this mainstream education may bring professionally trained people to Sami society, but does not necessarily secure understanding of how that society functions, nor does it secure that society from being a victim of turnover or the experimental field of young newly-trained specialists. In this respect one could say that the four universities, the five university colleges and the 26 state colleges do a good job.

In Norway, some of the professional schools have individually based enrollment of Sami students by special quotas. This enrollment has as its goal to promote enrollment of Sami students to training in certain professions, e.g. in general medicine, veterinary medicine, social worker training, journalist training, agriculture etc. For a long time the enrollment has been based on ethnic heritage. In recent years more and more Sami language mastery is being used in enrollment criteria. To some degree one could say this gives Sami students a better opportunity, on an individual basis, to get professional training beside the normal enrollment system. Since there is no claim of applying for a job in Sami society after graduating for those enrolled, the best possible result is that one is lucky who gets it, and the next best is that there, somewhere in the national system, will be a trained Sami professional, but for what purpose? To train individual Sami to different academic positions can of course be considered as a part of building a Sami society.

But it has its limits if the programs are not designed to train students for academic positions with relation to the society they are going to work in. So programs in general can be understood as being an aspect of better social opportunity for individuals to get post-secondary education. By the time it became possible for Sami to attend general programs the social pressure was may be so hard that they naturally applied for positions in the Sami society. But as society in general became more specialized the understanding of what a Sami could do and still be considered a Sami changed. It does not seem to be a necessary result that the graduation of a Sami increases the number of Sami professionals in the Sami society. It rather has an impact on individuals' careers.

A brief historical background

Sami post-secondary education can be considered as established at the first time by the years of 1750s when the missionary Thomas von Westen established *Seminarium Lapponicum* aimed at training young males to speak Sami language in the fight for consolidating and extending the expansion of Christianity among the Sami population. Courses in Sami studies have been arranged at the University of Oslo since 1848 (*The Sami People* 1990:141). Since then, education, including higher education has been a battlefield between those who consider education an instrument of assimilating the Sami into Norwegian society and those who consider education to be an instrument of strengthening and building a Sami society.

These days higher education, or post-secondary education, faces another kind of challenge: meeting diverse demands of different geographical areas where Sami live, post-secondary education is a part of the struggle and fight for modern Sami institutions. At the same time, established institutions defend their barricades. There are interesting perspectives to be aware of.

One could certainly ponder the concept Sami post-secondary education. Is it a concept that should cover specially designed program, in specially designed institutions with a certain structure for a certain population of students? Or, is it only a label on some kind of adjusted programs, aimed to cover some of the needs of professionally trained people within Sami society? Even the concept Sami society brings different perspectives to such a discussion. We can find a gap between those who really doubt if one can use such a concept in the Sami situation to politically stated aims and needs for strengthening Sami society.

Some examples of concepts used

Magga (1990) explains about Sami economy that it consists of economies corresponding with Sami ecological tradition in utilizing resources and that carry the Sami culture. He further gives examples of the traditional economies as agriculture, reindeer herding, fishing, hunting and other kinds of land utilization. But he also includes secondary and tertiary industries utilizing, or further processing, products of the primary industries. Some of these industries create a foundation for Sami society and culture in Sami settlement areas. Magga (1994) further refers to the Norwegian constitution that gives legitimacy to use of the concept "Sami social life," and further connects this to the concept Sami society.

Høgmo (1985) tries to find solutions to or perspectives on the concept of Sami labor. He explains some part of it by differentiating between the concept Sami in terms of given structures, and the concept Sami in terms of how people articulate themselves in daily life. Labor, as a cultural articulation, then, has to be considered through on one hand an existing documentable ecological cultural ecology, and on the other hand, how the work is expressed through single individuals' or group's concrete operation of activities.

The Norwegian government in its "white book" [i.e. Parliamentary report] relates the following on the concept Sami research p. 76 : "... primarily the research that is aimed to produce more knowledge about areas that are of special interest for Sami society, including language, religion, social relations, economy, ideology, history and history of law," (St.meld.nr.36). In the same white book it is further stated that there are needs for academic competence in fields other than those mentioned above, like natural science, medicine and management.

In these above mentioned examples we find distinct common perspectives that can be used to give meaning to the concept Sami education and research in many senses. It has to take into consideration both tradition and contemporary challenges, and it has to take into consideration both ethnicity and general academic challenges. It has to deal with individual, group and system-level aspects.

Political ideals

It is, in a Sami political sense, normal to consider the Nordic Sami Council's program as a kind of integrated solution for all-Sami political directions. The programs are adopted and approved by the Nordic Sami Conference, consisting of elected representatives from Sami organizations throughout the whole Sami area, Sapmi, now also including the Kola Peninsula in Russia.

The Sami education and school political program was adopted at the 14th Sami Conference in 1989. The principal aim (1989:18) the Conference stated: "We, the Sami have to get control over our own education and school politics and thus uphold and widen cultural self government. To govern the Sami education and schooling affairs there shall be organs set up by Sami themselves. These organs will govern the Sami education and school politics. Sami school administration must become a reality in all administrative levels, locally and at the Nordic level." Later in this program (*Sámiráddi* 1989) it is declared that: "School and education are important tools in building up the future Sami society." Further in the same program (1989:19): "To take care of higher education and research, a Sami institute for higher education must be established in connection with the Nordic Sami Institute. The Nordic co-operation must be strengthened in experiments, research and other schooling affairs."

If we consider the declarations as political ideals we then find that Sami control of the educational system seems to be a part of the concept of relevance. And as a part of this, we can further deduce that institutionalizing through Sami-controlled institutions is necessary to fulfill the demand of relevance, and this builds up a kind of reciprocity between the institutions and Sami governing bodies.

This model was used when the Nordic Sami Institute was established in 1973 as an "all-Sami"-institution. This Institute is funded by the Council of Nordic Ministers and is a research and cultural institute. So there is an example of an institution, but it is not a post-secondary training institute. But in the same program an integrated institute and post-secondary training institution, are proposed.

The Norwegian Sami Parliament's plan for 1994-97 states some central goals for Sami research and post-secondary education. Among the central goals of the Parliament's activities one can identify goals with direct relevance to the perspectives of Barnhardt & Kirkness and Hampton. The Parliament seeks ways to strengthen and maintain cultural continuity. As relevant subgoals to this we find:

- High level competence and satisfactory knowledge about Sami situation within society in general.
- Strong and dynamic Sami research and academic locations, and institutions conducting research on Sami situation.

- Develop a Sami education and training system that contributes to formalizing, improving and adjusting knowledge, skills, attitudes, norms and values within Sami society.
- Sami citizens with knowledge and values tied to a multicultural society (Sami Parliament 1994).

We further find it expressed that post-secondary education and research on Sami matters are central instruments in the maintenance and improvement of a Sami society based on Sami premises (*Sametingsplan* 1994-97). It is further stated that it is necessary to improve Sami educational programs and strengthen the research on Sami related conditions. Here we also find emphasis placed on the development of special enrollment conditions for Sami student recruits. Another central point is the establishment postgraduate programs in Sami environments. Research is of course mentioned as being important for Sami society, and it is necessary to have researchers in many disciplines, giving them better possibilities to qualify for disciplinary competence both within traditional Sami research areas, such as social science and culture, as well as in the field of natural science and medical research. The Sami Parliament claims as necessary the development of a separate white book on Sami research and post-secondary education, varied sources for recruiting people to academic positions and the necessity of having a jointly located Sami research and university campuses. If we compare this specific part of the Sami Parliament's plan with the Nordic Sami program we find a high degree of similarity in the political goals, the substance, and in the strategy of institutionalizing.

As we see, central focus is on relevance and reciprocity between post-secondary education and Sami society. We further find concepts such as respect of the culture and the society, contributing service to the people, and continuity of tradition. These could be translated being political ideals. Other central political documents concerning post-secondary education include the recent white book on post-secondary education (St.meld. nr. 40 1990-91). The Norwegian government states its special responsibility to lay down foundations that the Sami people can secure and maintain its language, culture and social life. It further states that the needs of Sami society should be the foundation of the content and organization of education and training. Here again we can identify responsibility, reciprocity and relevance as stated ideals. The committee on education in the Norwegian Parliament in its proposal (Innst.S. nr. 230, 1990-91) stresses special measures to increase the number of Sami students enrolled in post-secondary education. Mentioned are preparatory courses, enrollment by tests as alternative enrollment, scholarships etc.

An institutional example

The Sami College was established January 1, 1989 as a state operated college fully funded by the Ministry of Education to serve the needs of the Sami population in terms of teacher training for the Sami, and to operate under the cover of the Law of Teacher Training in Norway and the rules for operating Colleges of Education and Regional Colleges. During the planning and the implementing process it was early decided as one of the goals of the College to serve the whole Sami population in the Nordic countries. This has been done through agreements between the Ministries of Education, and has been in practice for many years already. The College itself can be defined as a local authority, because it has its local administration and a regional board. From August 1, 1994 it also has its College board elected locally.

The rules for operating the college through the different courses also specify guidelines for establishing networks for teaching practice in the three countries Norway, Finland and Sweden. The College hires its faculty from all these countries. Also the College, on behalf of several Universities and Regional Colleges, coordinates research symposia, seminars and exchanges across the borders. This also entails cooperation with the Nordic Sami Institute. It mainly focuses on language research, training and preservation, research on local traditions, customs as well as training, but also on local economy, development in society and more. Journalist training is also a good example of cooperation. The state authorities have strongly supported this by funding the College. The Norwegian Parliament has, by its subcommittee on Education, through its annual comments to the State budget, given support to this kind of cooperation between local authorities.

Corresponding initiatives in the United States and other places

In the United States the Tribal College Movement is understood as an initiative on behalf of higher education by and for indigenous people. These colleges have been established as a culturally based alternative, with the cultural link between college and community as a central ingredient in goals, philosophy as well as content. Central functions have been (Barnhard 1991) assisting communities with cultural revitalization, spiritual renewal, tribal development, self-government and other essentials to the process of community empowerment.

In this example, we find postulated that post-secondary institutions take part in and are linked to specific needs of community development. As some of these initiatives cover tribes as nations, the institutions also can be understood serving as national incitements. Their role ranges over a wide spectrum, from being tools to construct a nation-like common understanding, improving cultural identity, improving economy, sectors and regions, and seeking new knowledge and understanding.

Such foundations can be understood as a demonstration of liberty and developing a kernel of a nation's pure existence and creative power. This could be compared e.g. with the establishment of a Norwegian University as a part of the Norwegian nation building. As such, the university played a role in building a common understanding of what constituted the nation. Further, as a part of the Greenlandic Home Rule there has been established a Greenlandic University, *Ilisimatusarfik*. In other parts of the fourth world we find similar examples, the Maori people (New Zealand), Inuits (Canada). In these examples we find a commitment to the collective interests of the indigenous community, instead of mainly focusing on the individual.

The collective commitment as a strategy for post-secondary institutions must also have its parallel in the goal, substance and organizing of programs. If we convert the ideal at the institutional level to the substance of professional training, we find that the individuals subjective orientation as a Sami has to be completed with professional studies in cultural understanding and communication.

Cultural background vs. cultural understanding

Kvernmo & Stordahl (1990) describe an attitude among many Sami academicians that Sami background itself is a qualifing competence. The authors refer to an opinion postulating that a Sami masters all about the Sami situation, as they on the other hand describe as necessary for Sami academicians to develop cultural understanding and self reflection as instruments to be better professionals.

If we consider these ideas being professional ideals concerning Sami post-secondary education one could formulate several challenges. One obvious challenge for all situations is that post-secondary education has to have an analytic approach, not an ordinary training program with a "dash" of cultural garnish. This analytic approach could consist of cultural understanding and orientation towards a multicultural context involving improvement of the individuals' professional management. This of course, should not only include Sami students, but every professional student training for work in a multi-cultural society.

Identifying and organizing relevant and reciprocal priorities in Sami higher education

The Sami College is one of the post-secondary institutions established for the purpose of Sami education. The Sami College is from August 1, 1994 the reorganized Sami College, and is one of the new 26 State Colleges in Norway. By the funding of the Sami College since January 1, 1989 the Norwegian Government aimed to establish a college with special responsibility towards the Sami, not only in Norway, but also opening its programs towards the Sami in the whole of Sapmi. If we tie post-secondary education to research policy and cooperation I want to focus on two areas:

(1) - contemporary research policies
(2) - future focuses and cooperation.

Contemporary research priorities

In this part I am referring to the College priorities only in general, and I will aim to focus on the main principles of the College priorities. During the reorganizing process all the new 26 Colleges (reorganized from the former 98 Colleges) were asked by the Royal Ministry of Church, Education and Research to formulate the basic focuses of the college activities, covering both research and education programs. Since the funding of the college covers both research and education, the college found its basic idea of activities to be: "The Fountain of Sami Education."

The basic principle for all colleges activities is that education is based on research. Research is the basic foundation of the education programs, and the programs play an important role in distribution of research-based knowledge. In the case of our college this is defined as being an important part of building the Sami society by identifying, formulating, articulating and institutionalizing the latent knowledge of Sapmi among the Sami, both historically, contemporarily and with focus on the future.

One will not find these formulated accurately as stated by me, but they must be understood as my interpretations of the College strategic plan and the goals of the College. I will later exemplify some of them. If one compares the goals of the College with the political ideals of the Sami Parliament in Norway they will, to some degree, be compatible.

Since research priorities as we find them in operation in one institution do not give a valid or reliable picture with the needs of the entire society we have to seek for the arguments behind the priorities, and in this way compare the chosen priorities with the overall picture of present political aspects of the Sami case.

Then, what kind of arguments do we find behind the priorities in the case of the Sami College?

(i) Among the arguments based on international documents we find the ILO-convention no. 169, the European Council's charter on regional and less taught languages in Europe and the Agenda 21.

(ii) Among Norwegian national documents we find such as several reports from Norwegian Public Commissions (NOU 1988:42), white papers from the Norwegian government: (28:1991-92, 52:1992-93, 36:1992-93, 52:1992-93), report from a committee under Norwegian Research Council (NAVF 1990), and the Sami Parliament plan 1991-93. As well as the Norwegian Constitution, article 110 A.

All these documents named, to different degrees and from different perspectives, stress and state that it is the responsibility of the state authorities to:

–   lay the foundation for further development of Sami economy, culture and society...
–   recognize the Sami rights themselves to have a great impact on the basics for their own situation...
–   recognize that education and research are central areas of activities...

Beside this, and as the perspective of development and change, institutions of research and education have to take into consideration the balance between imported knowledge and the articulation of Sami society's own knowledge. This means the need to create an arena, or *the* arena, for change and transmission between scientific processes and the Samis' own knowledge that goes far beyond what one institution alone, or that single research fellows alone, or single programs alone are in position to manage.

From this point of view, our institution, even before the re-organization, faced the need of recruiting personnel on different levels. Both on the master degree level as well as for post-graduate level scholars. The next step, as necessary as the first one, was to seek means to fund education for researchers. Now, this brings us to the question of how to organize and how to structure the ongoing research.

Organization

The last years' discussion and dialogue about how to organize the college brought us to the conclusion of establishing two departments, namely the department of humanities and the department of pedagogy, social science and environment. Each single member of the faculty has his/her base in one of the departments depending on the kind of education programs one belongs to: However as you will see, the research activities cross the borders between the national programs.

The solution itself, in terms of organizing, is not by any means an original one, and reflects a more traditional way of thinking. If we compare it with the education programs, we find that teachers' training and kindergarten teacher training is organized by the department of pedagogy, social science and environment, but has some part of the program, for example language training and traditional craft training, organized by the department of humanities. The two-year traditional crafts program is organized by the department of humanities but is partly the responsibility both of pedagogy, even social science and environment. We could call this a disciplinary-based form of organization, but it has both an internal disciplinary base as well as an interdisciplinary function, since two or more disciplines are intimately involved in planning and operating the education. Themes in the education programs are often formulated from several views from several disciplines, and this has an impact on the research structure. This organization has to be compared with the research structure before we find a more explicit design.

Research structure

Based on the analyses of the needs of Sami society, the college decided to focus on three main areas of research.

(1) Language and language development

(2) Resource management and sustainable use of natural resources in Sapmi

(3) Sami education and understanding

These areas of research are aimed to focus on some of the areas that are critical both historically, contemporarily and in terms of future for the Sami people and for Sapmi. Research priorities are done within these areas, and within these we try to find both external funds and collaborators. In addition, our staff is motivated and guided by research advisors.

Our research advisors are senior research fellows with a high-level of competence and integrity on Sami research and research in Sapmi. This arrangement is funded by the Norwegian Research Council. Among many projects one could name Sami literature; comparison between traditional and chemical methods of preparation of reindeer hide; Sami knowledge, design and substance in southern-Sami ornaments. Further, traditions in Sami child-rearing, changes in traditional child-rearing, identity and changes of identity among elders in reindeer-herding, terminology in traditional craft, adolescence in some Sami communities, bilingual education, life-values, collectivity and elitism among reindeer-herders, thematics of aboriginality as an challenge for philosophy of law and theories of democracy.

Future focuses and cooperation

From my view point the future focus and cooperation should be based on some basic principles, but cooperation itself should be considered the crucial point.

1. Sami research needs to be based on the freedom to define, initiate and organize research, and the possibility to prioritize of what kind of research should be defined as Sami research, at least when using public funding.

(i) This principle calls for the need of a research policy-making body in Sapmi, based on cooperation within Sapmi's policy-making bodies in general and between these and Sami institutions.

(ii) This calls for an institutionalized process that we do not have in the present situation, consisting of negotiations between Sami political bodies and Sami institutions, between Sami political bodies and national state research funding systems, and the challenge for Sami institutions to survive during the competition with other research institutions.

(iii) This does not mean that we want to decrease the single researcher's possibility to have the freedom to decide what to focus on. But, as we are dealing with public priorities and public funding, we need both rather than only one or the other.

2. Sami research has to be carried out in a network of cooperation between Sami institutions both nationally as well as in the whole of Sapmi. Sami research further needs close international relations with indigenous research institutions, and with other institutions with strong support for aboriginal peoples.

Both 1 and 2, namely the basic principles and the network could be means used to secure that the knowledge reached through research is to the benefit of the aboriginal peoples . On the other hand the building of a network and other strong ties between institutions opens channels of communication that can be used for exchanges of many kinds.

References:

Sametinget 1994. *Sametingsplan for perioden 1994-97.*

Sámeráddi 1991. *The Sami Education- and Schoolpolitical Program,* Ohcejohka.

Kirke-, utdannings og forskningsdepartementet 1992-93. St.meld.nr. 36 *Forskning for fellesskapet.*

Kirke-, utdannings og forskningsdepartementet 1990-91. St.meld.nr. 40 *Fra visjon til virke Om høgere utdanning.*

Kirke-, utdannings og forskningsdepartementet 1989-90. St.meld.nr. 53 *Lærer-utdanning ved høgskoler og universitet.*

Kirke-, utdannings og forskningsdepartementet 1993-94. Ot.prp.nr. 85 *Om lov om høgere utdanning.*

Kommunal- og arbeidsdepartementet 1992-93. St.meld.nr. 52 *Om norsk same-politikk.*

Stortinget 1990-91. Innst.S.nr. 230 Innstilling fra Kirke-, og undervisningskomite-en om høgere utdanning, *Fra visjon til virke.*

Sámi instituhtta. 1990. *The Sami People,* Davvi Girji OS, Karasjok.

Barnhardt, Ray and Kirkness, Verna J. 1991. "First Nation and Higher Education," *Journal of American Indian Education* 30(3):1-15.

Høgmo, Asle. 1985. *Samisk arbeid hva er det?*, Draft. Pedagogisk forsknings-institutt, Universitetet i Oslo.

Magga, Ole Henrik. 1994. *Foredrag ved Utdanningskonferansen* 31.10-01.11. Guovdageaidnu/Kautokeino.

Magga, Ole Henrik. 1990. "Samiske næringer, en nødvendighet eller ikke?" *Fore-drag ved Næringspolitisk seminar for indre Finnmark* 7.-8.11.1990.

Barnhardt, Ray. 1991. "Higher Education in the Fourth World: Indigenous People Take Control," *Canadian Journal of Native Education,* Vol. 18:2.

John T. Solbakk

Sami Mass Media
– *Their Role in a Minority Society*

Introduction

In 1980, the year before the Norwegian government chose to send a police force of more than 600 men northwards to remove the demonstrators who were preventing the commencement of the building of the hydroelectric plant in Alta, the Sami resistance had also begun to find stronger modes of expression, not the least of which included adopting forms that were non-traditional even for the Sami movement. The first Sami hunger strike was conducted outside the Norwegian Parliament (Storting), something which, of course, created strong reactions among Sami spokesmen established in the Norwegian political system, but which also generated amazement and respect among many Sami. Many certainly now felt that the conflicts between the Sami and the Norwegian majority society were in the process of reaching a point where the Sami reactions against the Norwegian minority policies could get out of control. That year the largest independent Sami organization, Norgga Sámiid Riikkasearvi (Norwegian Sami National Association), NSR, arranged a large Nordic Sami media seminar in Alta with the topic of "Sami media's social responsibility." A Sami veteran within journalism expressed strong skepticism at the seminar to what he called the "doubtful journalistic practices" of "Sámi Áigi," the new (and only) Sami-language newspaper that two years earlier had come out with its first issue. I was editor of the newspaper at that time. It was his opinion that the newspaper and its editor had clearly taken sides in the current political conflict. In his opinion I had in an article quite clearly expressed that I favored the Sami party in the conflict with the authorities. Not taking sides had to be the guideline also for Sami journalistic undertakings, asserted my elder Sami colleague.

Scarcely a year went by before we again came to meet in Alta, many to demonstrate their opposition to the decision to build a 110 meter high dam for a large power plant in Alta, and we, 50 or so journalists from the entire Nordic region, to report some of the most dramatic events in recent Norwegian and Sami history. For quite a few of us who reported, it was nothing other than an example in a series of innumerable attacks against an indigenous people in the heart of their own territory, staged and directed by authorities far away. The same authorities who, outside the country's borders, were supposedly to be known for representing one of the most progressive and civilized democracies in the world. The same veteran Sami journalist, who over his entire journalistic life had worked for Norwegian newspapers with connections to the political party that had ruled throughout most of post-war Norway's history, approached me, clearly to unburden himself following a press conference at Alta Hotel. The press conference was held by police chief Einar Henriksen, leader for the army of policemen who were now well-prepared for action against the demonstrators at the river.

The police action came less than two days after the press conference, and resulted in a number of demonstrators – both Norwegian environmentalists and Sami nationalists – being arrested and later harshly fined for not having followed the police chief's orders to remove themselves from the site for the planned construction work. My Sami colleague, who naturally spoke Sami – but through his newspaper always had to report in Norwegian – virtually apologized for what he had expressed the previous year at our seminar. I hadn't forgotten our media seminar, but I was nonetheless somewhat surprised at my colleague's open admission of having been somewhat one-sided in his critique the year before. At the seminar in question I had also held a lecture on the topic "The Sami journalist's difficult double role as both defender and critic of Sami society." I had asserted at that time the Sami journalist's right, and maybe even duty, to defend Sami society in relationship to the majority society. My colleague now largely supported that opinion. The problem for him was that it was the Norwegian majority society that owned the media, and they ultimately determined what was important and correct information on Sami conditions.

In that which follows I will give the reader a little insight into Sami society through a short description of the Sami media situation, namely newspapers, radio and television, to which I will also direct a critical look at the undertakings of our media today. Even though the event described in the above introduction is taken from my time as a newspaper journalist, I want to hold myself first and foremost to radio, the medium which, with us, clearly controls the largest resources today. Where language is not expressly mentioned the discussion concerns Sami-language media, and at that the North Sami, which to a certain degree have developed a media presence. The same language, by the way, is spoken in Norway, Sweden and Finland.

Sami media today

Newspapers

Today we have two newspapers, *Áššu* and *Min Áigi,* which comes out twice a week. Both are published in Norway, with economic support from the Sami Parliament in Norway. *Áššu* is in its fourth year, while *Min Áigi* is a continuation of *Sámi Áigi,* which was founded in 1978. The newspapers have a subscription of somewhat more than a thousand for *Min Áigi,* and a little less for *Áššu.* The newspapers are probably read by more than five times as many people. Sami organizations are important owners of both newspapers, together with a number of private individuals and host townships, which are Sami-majority townships. *Áššu* was founded as a so-called cultural newspaper with a feature style as a goal, in order not to be a direct competitor with the already established news-newspaper *Min Áigi.* Subsequently *Áššu* has become more of a newspaper containing both news and sports reporting. Because of choices on content material the newspaper is identified more as a local paper for the townships where it is published. *Min Áigi,* on the other hand, strives to be a newspaper for the entire Sami area where North Sami – the dialect possibly spoken or understood by 75 percent of those who can speak or understand Sami – is spoken. The paper therefore has correspondents in more Sami townships, also in Finland. However, there are still none in Sweden, where the newspaper is also read. Plans exist to make the newspaper a daily.

Periodic publications

Sweden and Finland do not have their own Sami newspapers. In Finland there is a magazine called *Sápmelaš* which comes out once a month with between 24 and 32 pages. This magazine is also read over the entire North Sami area, but *Sápmelaš* doesn't have a circulation of more than a thousand either. The magazine prints both shorter, topical news articles and thematic issues. The latter are often the products of pupils and teachers at Sami schools. In Sweden the monthly *Samefolket* has been published continuously since the 1920s, but then in Swedish. In recent years the magazine has regularly had articles in Sami too. These magazines also receive economic support from cultural funds in their countries of publication.

In Norway a children's magazine and a youth magazine are also published, both quarterlies. Because of low circulation these publications are also dependent on economic support from the Sami Parliament, administered by the Sami Cultural Council.

Books

Independent Sami publishing activity has developed during the last 20 years. But economic support from state cultural and educational funds has also been a necessity for Sami book publication. In Norway the funds for Sami book publishing are today under Sami administration. The Sami Cultural Council, appointed by the Sami Parliament, administers the fund for literary publications, including children's books, while the fund for school books is controlled by the Sami Education Council. In Sweden and Finland arrangements for the financing of, among other things, book publications, have also eventually been established, corresponding to what the Sami in Norway have had for nearly 20 years. But there are still large discrepancies between the three Nordic countries in regards to, among other things, the financing of book publications. The problem is nevertheless not so great that it prevents many Sami authors in Sweden and Finland from publishing their books through Sami publishers in Norway, as financing arrangements are better here. The downside is that this has until now functioned as a cushion for the governments in Stockholm and Helsinki in matters regarding appropriations to support for Sami language and culture in these countries.

Today 25 to 30 Sami titles are published annually, mostly school books. Issues average 1000 for each title. Most of the books are published in Norway, but also read and used in the other countries.

Others

A Norwegian-language newspaper is accepted as a member of the Sami Newspaper and Book Publisher Association, namely *Ságat*. The newspaper has a turbulent 40-year history. Eighteen years after its founding in 1956 it was taken over in 1974 through a buy-out by forces within the Norwegian Labor Party in Finnmark. That was also the occasion for the establishment of the independent Sami newspaper *Sámi Áigi* in 1978. Since 1974 *Ságat* has been in opposition to the leading Sami organization, NSR, by, among other things, appearing as a mouthpiece for different organizations which have emerged, or by acting as a counterbalance to NSR itself. Today the newspaper has toned down its attacks against NSR and those who advocate Sami autonomy more, largely because forces which the newspaper has associated with have also accepted the establishment of an elected Sami body, and have even taken an active part in political work through the Sami Parliament. *Ságat* also receives press financial support, though not as a Sami-language organ. The newspaper argues today for reception of the same "Sami" press support as the Sami-language newspapers, with the argument that it too stands for the "Sami spirit." A large majority in the Sami Parliament, made up of NSR and independent representatives, in a resolution in the spring of 1996 elected not to equate Norwegian-language and Sami-language newspapers in matters pertaining to Sami press support today. The Labor Party's delegation voted in favor of *Ságat.*

Among "others" which must also be named is the rather inconspicuous religious monthly magazine "Nuortanaste." Inconspicuous because it in no way is pretentious, as it confines itself to simple black-and-white bursts and largely prints material of a religious nature. It must be named first and foremost for its long and unbroken history which goes back to 1898. The magazine has always had its faithful readership, never more than 1000 subscribers, but certainly many, many times as many readers. That must especially have been the case during the hardest periods of Norwegianization, from the beginning of the 1920s to the first decade after the last war, when the Sami didn't have any official mouthpiece. This small magazine has therefore also functioned at times as a little breathing hole for the never-completely-dead thought of Sami independence. Today the magazine plays a more modest role in Sami society.

Radio and television

The national radio and television companies in Norway, Sweden and Finland have their own Sami divisions, with their own administrations, studios and broadcast locales in areas of Sami concentration, respectively in Kárášjohka/Karasjok (Norway), Giron/Kiruna (Sweden) and Anár/Inari (Finland). All expenses are therefore also paid by the national companies, which are in turn financed through license fees from listeners and viewers. The Sami divisions have long called themselves Sami Radio, but have only in recent years gotten a degree of autonomy. The least progress has in this case also been made in Sweden. The Sami Radios have over time developed good cooperation, and the broadcasts are today organized in such a way that most can be received in the other countries. This functions particularly well between the Sami Radios in Norway and Finland. When the national companies plan to have a separate radio channel for only Sami broadcasts open in two to three years, the three Sami Radios are projected to jointly broadcast 12 to 16 hours in Sami per day, as opposed to 4 to 6 hours now. In Norway the radio broadcasts run weekdays from 7:30 to 9 am, then from 12:03 to 12:30 pm, and from 2 to 5:30 pm. Of these 330 minutes that can be received in Norway, Giron broadcasts 30 minutes in the morning and Anár 60 minutes during the afternoon. The rest comes from Kárášjohka.

TV broadcasts in Sami are understandably a rarity. Today Sami children are offered 30 minutes a week, one broadcast early Monday afternoon with a re-run on Sundays. There is a monthly half-hour for adults, also broadcast in the early afternoon. No improvement on the offering has been announced for the near future. The TV offerings aren't any better in any of the other countries in which the Sami live.

The Alta case – a turning point

I will not assert that it is on the basis of thorough studies that I rest my opinion that a remarkable change in attitude and practice also occurred among many Norwegian journalists with regard to their reporting on Sami conditions, precisely because of the struggle over the Alta/Kautokeino hydroelectric project in the 70s, which was handled by the Norwegian authorities by bringing in large police forces from the south. It was later, by the way, revealed that sending in military units against the opponents of the building of the hydro-electric plant was also considered, but that the idea was dropped out of a fear that it would lead to a deep split of both the government and the Labor Party.

I believe that there is a good foundation for drawing conclusions like the ones indicated above, not least because interest in the struggle over the hydroelectric project after the event has primarily focused on the Sami political perspective. In any event there is no reason to doubt that the perspective of Sami journalists who worked in Norwegian media gained another dimension, and had an effect on their journalistic activities. Just as it also happened with my previously mentioned colleague. Changes also gradually occurred within the Norwegian media institutions in such a way that one can justifiably speak of "before and after the Alta case" in recent Norwegian journalism in relationship to Sami conditions.

I further believe, and it can be one of my hypotheses here, that there first occurred within Norwegian journalism a slow revolution in opinions towards the Sami minority from the end of the 70s and through the 80s, and only after that did slow stirrings begin within the ruling party in Norway, and that finally the new winds reached the party's forums furthest north in the country. We are talking about the Norwegian Labor Party. The causes for the changes in attitudes within the party in the northernmost county can surely be sought many places, not just as indicated above in the pressure which necessarily emanated from the central party apparatus, but also because the party in the north still had some articulate and well-arguing Sami members. Even if the description above can be seen to represent a simplification of a more complex cause-and-effect relationship, it is my opinion that it can serve as a good example for illustrating what influence and power the media ultimately can represent. Nevertheless, my most important point here is the following: The media's focusing on Sami conditions, no longer as before through bulletins of a sensational and exotic character, but rather through a somewhat more nuanced reporting (of course, we are far from what we can call a balanced and complete coverage in Norwegian media of what happens in Sami society), has given us Sami a little breathing space in the midst of the feeling of being on the way towards loosing the remains of our Saminess. In this space some small Sami revolutions have taken place, not sharp and dramatic as upheavals often are, but gradual and often quiet. Unfortunately we must also admit that far too much silence has reigned over areas which shouldn't remain quiet, for example over the question of what kind of Sami society it is that we desire for ourselves in the future.

The media's undertakings

The sought-after Sami social debate

I am here only going to occupy myself with that which has happened within sections of the media sector, in such a way that I will not get into the results of – if there is a real content to the assertion – the quieting of the Sami social debate after the conflict over the Alta/Kautokeino hydroelectric project was lost. The following occurred in the wake of the lost conflict: The government acted on NSR's suggestion to define the Sami's rights. Two committees were appointed, one to address cultural questions and one to address political rights and the right to land and water. Culture and politics were, relatively, not very controversial questions, particularly after the government had established an elected Sami body which had only an advisory function with no veto power. On the other hand it has been more difficult to reach a result in regards to the Sami's rights to the land in their own area. The committee gave a final opinion in January 1997, after 16 years. During all these years nearly the entire Sami society sat silently and waited for an answer to the fundamental question of land-tenure rights. It appears as if everyone has believed that the so-called Sami Rights Commission would provide an answer to the question of who is the rightful owner of land and water in Sami areas, and therefore have loyally waited for the Committee to finish its work. As information leaked out from the Committee during the last few years which was nothing that we

Sami could be satisfied with, an awakening finally occurred. Now a number of Sami organizations have come out with declarations that it is we Sami who have the original rights, but what we now await is a plan for the administration of the Sami area that protects our interests in a better manner than previously.

My question regarding the lengthy silence on central questions in our own society is precisely if our media have played a decisive role here, or if they haven't played the role the media should have played. I am thinking not only of questions regarding rights to land and water, but also the development of the language, and the discussion of the lack of education among Sami, the meager media offerings. I understand quite clearly that all the Sami who are able to speak and write publicly bear their share of responsibility for the debate which has not been initiated concerning the above-mentioned questions. I nevertheless believe that the very media we ourselves have been involved in establishing must have derailed at some point. It simply cannot be denied that the resources that have been employed in the establishment of our media have not met the expectations we had. Only a couple of years ago the president of the Norwegian Sami Parliament ventured to point out the clear lack of professionalism in the journalistic media institutions, and hopefully some took this to heart. We have nonetheless not seen great progress in the development of the profession, not just as a bad copy of Norwegian media, but rather adjusted to the particular demands a long oppressed minority society has regarding the transmission of information to its own citizens.

I believe that one can, in a description of a minority society in relationship to the surrounding majority society, easily express that these two societies are in many ways at different stages of development. The minority society, depending on the degree of oppression over time, will lag behind. An area where this is evident is the disparate educational levels within the majority and the minority. A common factor for many ethnic minorities is also the fact that the level of knowledge is quite low in the area of one's own history, language, and one's own cultural background in general. This of course has the simple explanation that it is the majority population's history and culture with its adherent fields that have been the educational subjects in school for the minority as well, and not the minority and its own history. When our Sami media, then, lacking a deeper awareness of this fact, begin to copy our larger neighbors' modes of operations, these media cannot become anything else than extremely bad copies of these, and in any event of little service as instruments in an information service for the minority.

The "radical" Sami leader

In the spring of 1994, the leader of the NSR (Norwegian Sami National Association), Nils Thomas Utsi, broke the long-standing silence on the problem of rights. In order to finally spark a public exchange of opinion he spoke out at a Nordic Sami Council meeting in Kiruna in May 1994 about how he could imagine the problems of rights being solved in practice in the northernmost county in Norway, where the State claims to be the single owner of the land. The essence of his message was that he saw the majority of the population of Finnmark as being of Sami descent, and thereby entitled to partake in the election of representatives to the Sami Parliament, providing they themselves desired to do so. After this it shouldn't be any sort of democratic problem to transfer the administration of all the State's land in Finnmark to the Sami Parliament. The matter was given extensive coverage in both Sami and Norwegian newspapers, still without emphasizing the idea of power tranference, but there was, in my opinion, an implicit challenge to both deadlocked methods of thinking relative to giving us Sami more power in our own house.

The one ingrown mode of thought is represented by the establishment which is to say the Norwegian administrative system of today, which up to now has also been deployed to protect the indigenous people interests in all areas. The leaders within this group are, however, Norwegian, most of them descendants of immigrants over the period of a couple hundred years (but naturally today not completely without Sami blood in their families), and descendants of Sami who are Norwegianized, and who today do not want to recognize their Sami origins. The challenge to perhaps the majority in this category lies primarily in that they must recognize their Sami origins in order to be able to participate in the Sami democratic decision-making process. For many this is simply an impossibility. In particular this applies to those who have fought persistently their entire lives to rid themselves of the stamp of inferiority that being Sami has always been for them. When they have nearly succeeded in wiping away the last remnants of traces, such as the clearly foreign sound in their Norwegian language – which is a give-away for most people – then they are met with the ghosts of the past, the heritage they have wanted to eradicate in order to be accepted as "of equal value" as all other good Norwegians in the kingdom. In some Sami villages where the Sami language is being made visible today through road and place signs also in Sami, the Sami signs are being removed and have been shot at with firearms. What hidden dark and aggressive feelings lie behind such actions? Perhaps psychiatrists would cautiously characterize this as "projected self-contempt." The braver ones have openly, through the media, dared to fight against the making visible of that which is Sami in their township. If these individuals are confronted with the fact that they live in a Sami township, their attitude is often that there were Sami here before, but not now. One can be quite certain that the grandparents, if not the parents, of the most rabid anti-Sami spokesmen of today were Sami-speaking.

The other group challenged by Utsi was his own, that is, the leading forces within the pro-Sami movement represented first and foremost by the NSR, and those who sympathize with it. This group has had the majority in the elected Sami Parliament in the two first electoral periods, and also makes up the 5-member Sami Parliament Council in its entirety. The challenge to the Sami Parliament, and especially to its majority, lies primarily in the fact that a quick expansion of the electorate for the Parliament could change the balance of power to NSR's disadvantage. What would result from that is that the Sami demands for the right to land and water, a future Sami autonomy, and equal status for Sami language and culture, could be watered down to nothing. Norwegianized Sami, even with seats in the Sami Parliament, would hardly view such goals as important. Thereby the Sami Movement's long-term goals would achieve bankruptcy in a so-called democratically elected Sami body. The winner in such a situation would be the assimilationist policy the Norwegian authorities have stood for throughout this century, and which they officially gave up only recently. In the meantime discrimination against everything Sami is rooted securely in large portions of both the Sami and the Norwegian populations, and institutionalized in the Norwegian administrative system. Outbreaks of self-contempt as described above are only one of many expressions of what generations of oppression have done to many Sami. This is a well-known phenomenon among other peoples in similar situations, but one must nevertheless not draw the conclusion that linguistic affiliation necessarily dictates one's political affiliation. One can surely find just as many Sami "nationalists" today among non-Sami speakers as among those who speak the language. And there should not be any doubt either that the Sami nation's future depends on Sami belonging to both language groups.

Into this complicated Sami landscape I would like to toss a Welsh quote on comparable oppositional relationships between Welsh-speaking and non-Welsh-speaking Welshmen, and here make the observation applicable to Sami conditions as a suitable summation:

> To sum up, one needs, whether discussing writers or people in general, to be able to separate patterns of cultural prosperity and decadence and disintegration – which undoubtedly exist and put certain limitations on the individual – from that individual's innate capacity to find a way out. In Wales this distinction is not always made, and English-speakers sometimes detect and resent a sense of superiority in the Welsh-speaker.

But fortunately there is another element, increasingly present in the Welsh-speaker's attitude, which overcomes any condescension: this is the consciousness that any future Wales and the Welsh language may have, must depend very largely on the English-speakers in Wales. (Ned Thomas 1973 and 1991: 117)

In this Sami landscape our media should, among other things, contribute with information – preferably both in Norwegian and Sami. No easy task, it must be admitted, but it is permissible to place strict demands on the media to ensure that the right information gets out, and misunderstandings and myths are deprived of life? This was also followed up by the Sami Radio, the only channel that reaches most Sami listeners. The impression I believe most radio listeners were left with after a news broadcast based on the newspaper report and a short interview with Nils Thomas Utsi was that we were again faced with one of his "radical" political initiatives. In connection with the newspaper report, precisely the term "radical" – read "extremist" – was the reporter's introduction to the issue; "if he hadn't now presented a far too radical proposal which actually only scared everyone." I have so far not registered any further or deeper follow-up to this topic in the radio, which is still our most important Sami news transmitter.

Sami media today also use what one can call a journalism of oppositions, particularly in news and topical broadcasts. My point is not that one shouldn't use the journalistic techniques one has at one's disposal, but that like any dangerous tool in the hands of "amateurs," this "method of oppositions" will most often lead to a poor result, evaluated from the point of view of the information value of the result. The reporters seem to blindly believe in, and therefore live according to, the rule that by bringing two opposite poles in front of a microphone they have the foundation for a good radio broadcast. To a degree they may be right, it can be good radio if the criterion is that the temperature in the studio is the measure of a good or bad radio broadcast. I fear that this type of radio unfortunately leads to the issue itself fading into the background, information about what the issue actually concerns is subordinated and in reality disappears in the noise around the microphone. Norwegian radio and TV journalists, for example, say straight out to the debaters they invite into the studio that they want the temperature up, and the debaters should naturally contribute to that end. It is, among other things, this type of journalism our Sami media have adapted directly. I can't see that it actually belongs here in the same form. Our tradition is to speak out about difficulties. Our people have always used time to illuminate an issue, a tradition that goes back to the earlier Sami social organization, called the *siida,* a term which can also be translated as "a local community." The siida had a gathering where one discussed current problems until a consensus was reached. There were no votes. Therefore discussions could also last several days. One finds some remnants of this in Sami reindeer herding circles today. I would like to underscore that important issues cannot be directed by the media's hurried and temperature-seeking approach. Can one imagine Sami media adjusting themselves to another reality than that which seems to rule in the media world? Yes, I would answer, if Sami society really chooses to do so.

Our discussed leader, who in my opinion tried to get a debate going concerning an important and difficult issue for a number of ethnic groups in the Sami area, appeared, in the memories of radio listeners at any rate, as a controversial and radical Sami politician severely diminishing the impact of his message. His outstanding initiative towards debate was drowned by the radio in stereotypes expressions used about people with opinions which cause listeners to distance themselves from the start, and not to concern themselves with approaching the real content. In a Sami society of conservative values one can easily, through placing a characterization such as radical on a leader, isolate him or her from the mainstream of accepted views within the organization and thereby put an end to that person's career as a leader. In part, I would say, that is what happened to Utsi. True enough, he had already then expressed a desire to be relieved of his duties at the coming national convention, half a year after the interview mentioned, but such announcements from a leader must also be seen as a question to the organization's members about a potential renewal of confidence. The media's coverage of the issue, in addition to Utsi's challenge to his own organization to make an unbiased reevaluation of the EU question from a Sami perspective, before the Norwegian referendum and after Sweden and Finland had joined, led to no direct appeals coming to him to continue. The leader desired a more thorough evaluation of the consequences for the Sami if the Sami in Norway remained outside EU while the Sami in Sweden and Finland were inside. Had anyone hoped for a debate about important question's in today's Sami society after the leader's play to the media, it would have to be said that the media themselves contributed to something completely different, primarily a debate over how much the sitting leader was suited to continue as leader of the largest Sami organization. The actual issue was drowned in others that were in reality less important. I believe that Nils Thomas Utsi deserves a better legacy as leader of the organization than merely a one-sided negative stamp such as that with which the term radical is unfortunately burdened.

The politicians or the media as establishers of premises?

When I have written above that our media frequently make use of polarizations in their method of informing, I would again like to emphasize that I am not a warm supporter of this method. I doubt that it is useful as a method for spreading information as it is employed today. The approach invites the creation of more oppositions than there actually are in the real world. Of course real disagreement arises in a living society concerning the political issues of the day, which the media are compelled to follow up on. Nonetheless not all issues are of such a nature that they need to be painted with a controversial brush, even if they are political issues, if the media's intention is primarily to shed light on the issues. It must still be much more important to enlighten readers and listeners concerning an issue's background conditions, its real content, instead of merely focusing on the fact that people are opposing each other. In any case it should be such that the core of the issue is something other than that two parties are in disagreement.

The media's hunt for oppositions also leads to our Sami politicians having to play up to the media's need for heated topics. The Sami Parliament's plenary sessions can serve as a good example here. At the opening of every session the opposition, primarily the Norwegian Labor Party's Sami Parliamentary delegation, has presented a scathing critique of the governing majority. To put it mildly, one must unfortunately say that the factual content of the criticism has seldom been in reasonable proportion to the use of rhetoric from the speaker's chair. For their part the media have adjusted themselves to this and wait with eager anticipation at the session opening to find out what the Labor Party's delegation will bring up this time. At the last session before Christmas in 1995 the leader of the group at the time was relieved. Maybe it was a sign that there too it was seen that the opposition should perhaps find other methods for advocating their politics, if they disagree with the assembly's majority in the first place. Then one hears, of course, criticism from the politicians in the Sami Parliament, most recently in the winter of 1996, from both the Sami Parliament's president Ole Henrik Magga, of NSR, and from the outgoing opposition leader Steinar Pedersen, that the media were far too caught up in the small disagreements that there actually are within the Sami Parliament about the fundamental questions facing Sami society. But it is also important to remind the politicians that they themselves are involved to the highest degree in creating such oppositions where they see a short term gain to their own advantage – which may manifest itself next time in the elections to a new Sami Parliament.

My concern is – and it can be repeated to the point of boredom

– that our media will not become anything other than very bad copies of the Nordic media they often emerge from, or which the Sami media have as their models. It is also my concern that in the competitive situation in which they find themselves, not competition between Sami media – which is more than welcome – but competition with superior Nordic media for their Sami readers' and listeners' attention, that they will more and more resort to the same devices and methods as the ever more commercialized Nordic media use in the hard-nosed competition in which they are daily immersed. The Sami media also seek attention, and the methods are big stories – preferably exposés of one sort or another. Now and then we notice strong reactions on the part of the newspaper-reading and radio-listening Sami audience against this form of journalism. It would be desirable that these reactions be taken seriously by the media. I don't think they are merely an expression of a desire to speak on behalf of one side in an issue.

Positive tendencies

Now I have drawn a far too one-sided picture of the Sami media world, one could object. Yes, but it is not an incorrect picture. I will nevertheless balance that picture somewhat in the continuation. Let me first give praise to the same NRK Sami Radio that I have primarily directed criticism against above. Precisely for its handling of the above-mentioned Rights Commission and its work – when still missing conclusions – the radio deserves a salute. True enough, more than half a year went by after Nils Thomas Utsi's initiative in the Norwegian local newspaper before Sami Radio began broadcasting leaks from the Commission's work. The Commission's members bear the duty to remain silent about their work and negotiations. The radio has nonetheless been able to present concrete and detailed information from the Commission, even concerning majority and minority groupings. Finally the general Sami public got to know that the Sami representatives in the Commission, who are of course in the minority, want to advance clear minority opinions and proposals that can be more acceptable to the Sami conception of rights pertaining to the management of land and water than that which applies today. This is even more important for those who in the future will continue to assert the indigenous peoples' rights, that this Commission does not have any solution to the demands that the Sami have posed and are posing to the Norwegian authorities concerning our traditional title rights to our own area. Thereby 16 years of self-imposed waiting in silence have been wasted. Now Sami politics must finally be formulated for the next generations of Sami, but it will also need to pay necessary attention to the other ethnic groups that have lived in the Sami area for several generations, and this must most likely be done without noteworthy attention to the Rights Commission's majority and minority opinions. We can hope that this doesn't come as a shock to our political leaders and their organizations, because of the Sami radio's exposé of the commission's work. Of course there will always be reason to criticize our media, but here at any rate the Sami radio showed that it has a potential, that it has resources that can be employed, and not least that it also has some of the necessary competence and the necessary courage to dig up and expose where there is true need for it.

I shall continue with a little more praise to the same institution. NRK Sami Radio is one of the institutions where a quiet revolution has taken place over the last 10 to 15 years. The institution deserves a salute for the relatively quick building up which has occurred, considering the shortage of resources Sami society suffers from in regards to competence in most areas in society. The technical and material building up has taken place in understanding with and with prioritized support from the leadership of the central NRK administration.

New program policy – finally an activist radio?
With the establishment of the more independent Sami editorial staff in Karasjok from 1976 onward, both the leadership in Oslo and the

staff saw it necessary to have a program policy fixed in the form of written text. The final text would have to be carefully formulated, a sort of compromise but nonetheless sufficiently open in relation to that which we viewed as the radio's mission, i.e. to be an active element in the development of Sami culture and society, under the assumption that we would fulfill the same role in relation to Sami society as that which NRK fulfilled in relation to Norwegian society. The program policy leaves, for that matter, no doubt that we were to be defenders of Sami language and culture, but we were all the same not supposed to be some sort of Sami activist radio, according to the views of the "watchdogs." Among other things the radio was possibly seen as a necessary evil; we were harmless as long as we only occupied ourselves with language and culture and didn't make politics out of it. How could an oppressed nation's radio channel avoid making even such questions, which were non-threatening for the majority, into controversial political questions? If we didn't have the ability to make the daily general Sami activities into a political question at a higher level, then it is my opinion that we wouldn't have done our job as a radio channel that was to be a mouthpiece, a builder of better self-understanding, one that could participate in giving back to our own belief in Sami values. Of course this would have to lead to collisions with the established majority interests.

Today, 20 year after the relocation of the small Sami editorial staff to Karasjok, one can say that NRK's Sami Radio is more like the activist radio that a local newspaper feared in the fall of 1976. In any case it is such on paper, because today NRK Sami Radio's mission statement reads:

> NRK shall in the coming years be one of the most important tools in the preservation and development of Sami society. NRK has therefore set the following as long-term goals for its programming activity: Main goal: NRK shall in its programming activity participate in working so that the Sami can and will want to be Sami. (NRK Sami Radio long-term plan, approved by NRK's board Aug. 25, 1992)

Carefully expressed one must say that the radio has a clearly expressed Sami nationalistic goal. But this must be understood as being positively meant, and not in any way meant as a threat for other ethnic groups and cultures. In addition to a clearly expressed Sami nationalistic policy, the Sami radio within NRK has received a higher organizational connection to the mother organization. Thus it begins to resemble an administrative system with extensive inner autonomy, though still tied to NRK, whose board is appointed by the government. Because of these two relationships, its Sami nationalistic policy and the independence it is allowed, it is tempting to use a perhaps worn out image and say that the earlier opponents of too much freedom to the Sami "extremists" must have turned many times in their graves during recent years because of the large changes we have been witness to.

Part of the development also includes, of course, the regular increase of broadcast time and the number of employees. I do not, however, feel that an increase of editorial staffing over 15 years from 1980 to 1995 of 300 percent is especially impressive, considering the challenges that the radio, despite everything, has faced and faces. The number of journalists employed today is 20, of which 5 to 6 are engaged in one hour's TV production per month. The radio journalists have to cover 3 to 4 hours daily. Such quantitative information is perhaps not so interesting, however it could be more interesting if one dared to say something about the quality of the programs the listeners are offered. I have earlier indicated, with reference to the professional job two reporters have done in connection with the exposé of the secretive work of the Sami Rights' Committee, that there is a potential here. Nevertheless I would venture to assert that, compared with periods the radio has experienced with far fewer human resources, the broadcasts' quality today is not proportional to the increase of resources. The radio today has more journalists who are perhaps more professional than earlier, it has broadcasts that can sound more professional than earlier, but all the same I look for – not least in relation to the broadcast time the radio has at its disposal today – a qualitatively better content to the broadcasts. Here it is a question of how the resources are used. My impression is that the institution has prioritized quantity over quality. It is also my conviction that as long as the Sami Radio's program concept resembles NRK's district broadcasts to the point of confusion, with some adjustments from the national radio, where more or less all journalists are expected to be able to do the whole spectrum of programs, a large portion of the broadcast time will be filled with entertainment. The journalists are given the responsibility for filling a specific number of minutes with a certainly reasonable frame as a point of departure, but the talent unfortunately doesn't always stretch far enough.

What I am looking for in the broadcasts of today can be expressed with the following question: Where are the well-educated Sami social scientists? Where are the Sami historians – the only ones in the Nordic countries who have really dared to pose questions to the history writing which has been done up to now? Where are all the Sami linguists, economists, pedagogues, social pedagogues, and all the other professionals who could share with us the knowledge they have acquired through years of education? And of course there is reason to look for the traditional, the experienced Sami knowledge represented by those who have had it handed down to them from earlier generations. Shouldn't these be heard on the radio? What I would like to suggest to the radio institution here is that it should now specialize its programming activities such that different staffs or departments receive responsibility for their own fields. The well-known journalistic, the generalists, who are most often on the surface of an issue can be distinguished co-workers, but there is a limit to what they can be used for in a radio that despite everything is supposed to make it possible that "Sami can and will want to be Sami," as it is phrased in the institution's program policy.

It is certainly true that radio's role has changed over time and appears to change more rapidly today in competition for the audience's attention with, among others, the motion picture and electronic media. The role of radio can easily become that of the entertainer and the quick relayer of news. However weightier programs are still not completely abandoned. Our neighbors, the Norwegians, have enough radio channels to include them for the especially interested. But the Sami do not have the multitude of channels, rather still only a few hours a day – and then in competition with radio channels which the large majority of Sami can make use of. The language is no longer a barrier, at any rate not for the generation after the last war. That radio's role changes among the majority doesn't have to mean that the same thing must happen among us. I have earlier mentioned the difference in the general level of knowledge among the majority and the minority. Here I believe that we must, in the situation of media shortage in which we find ourselves, be able to demand that radio adapts itself to the task of producing and broadcasting programs with knowledge for both adults and children. It must also, to a much greater degree than today, be able to make us stop for reflection. I must, with apologies, admit that it is very seldom that the Sami radio has contributed to exactly that with this listener; unfortunately it has more often created a strong irritation because of the "noise" that all too often surrounds the broadcasts and hinders a potential message from reaching the listener.

Not too long ago I listened to a surprise change in a series of informal morning lectures from the Sami radio in Giron (Kiruna), Sweden. The morning broadcasts start at 7:30 am from Karasjok; Giron takes over at 8:00 am, and the broadcast returns to Karasjok and 8:30 am. I felt that the content in the lectures represented the type of reflection that I, among others, miss. This type of brain food at the start of a day could gladly be a permanent aspect of radio, at least in addition to the often formless morning ramblings we hear today. It seems, unfortunately, to have been a singular occurrence. I know that the lectures were offered to NRK Sami Radio in Karasjok, the Sami radio with the largest resources, but they didn't want to pay what the lecturer thought that he ought to be paid for the series. Kiruna, on the other hand, was willing. I think this tells something very clearly about the actual policy of the radio, or lack thereof. It seems to be other things that one puts a higher price tag on than a program with a qualitatively richer content. It could be that someone in the institution has sat too long in their position of leadership.

I believe that the institution already has thought in the direction of a subject-based division of the editorial staff, something that hopefully will also turn out to be realized when the radio gets its own channel at its disposition in a couple of years. The prioritizing up to today can surely be defended by the institution, and also be explained in that the institution and the programs only reflect Sami society as it is. I believe nonetheless that the definitively largest Sami media institution must stretch itself a good deal in order to at all be able to begin to approach the fulfillment of the intentions it has set for its activities.

TV

I have almost come to the end of my article without mentioning the most important medium, TV. That can be most easily explained by the fact that we in reality don't have Sami TV. What should one say about something that doesn't exist? A few self-evident things must nevertheless be mentioned. The first is that without getting started with daily Sami-language TV broadcasts as soon as possible NRK Sami Radio and TV (as the institution presents itself in the few monthly half hours it has received from NRK TV) will lose the attention of the Sami television viewers. I do not believe one will have taken a particularly long stride in the direction of reaching the earlier mentioned over-arching goal if the strongest medium is not utilized. No one would today characterize a monthly half hour in Sami for adults as TV broadcasts, not even for a linguistic minority. The same can be said about the weekly half hour for Sami children. You don't need to be knowledgeable in majority/minority relations in order to understand that these programs hardly have a purpose. Ask Sami parents how many of the weekly half hours their children absorb. I am afraid the answer will be that at least the smaller children often forget the weekly offer. Conscientious parents – and Sami parents must be just that to a much higher degree than Norwegian parents if, for example, the children are not to become completely alienated in relationship to their Sami heritage – often help with both remembering and motivating. By then the children have discovered other things to occupy them just when the Sami children's program is on. Should one then interrupt the game, for example, and more or less drag them to the TV, a device that one generally would like to see children spending less time watching? A continuation of today's media offering, or, more correctly, lack of media offering, will unfortunately lead to our people quickly being assimilated, quicker than perhaps is advisable from a psychological point of view. The Sami TV medium must unfortunately still be characterized today as a curiosity.

Ten years ago I was in Oslo, in the departmental offices that, among other things, distribute licenses for the starting up of local radio and television broadcasts. I did this errand for a local Sami association in Tana. The association wanted to start local radio broadcasts in Sami. The one in charge in the department offered a surprising challenge. Why didn't we apply for a license to start up local television broadcasts? Of course, that's exactly what we would have done if the township's 3000 inhabitants had lived in a couple of city blocks as in a suburb in Oslo, instead of spread out over a river valley of 250 km. No, I couldn't give any other answer than that we were waiting for NRK Sami Radio to also become NRK Sami TV. We have so far no knowledge of any other method of financing such things, and neither did the department manager. Unfortunately it is still like that.

At NRK Sami Radio and the Sami Parliament's joint seminar in November, 1995, where I was invited to present a few thoughts on the Sami radio's role in society, and where some of that which has been written above was presented, I also presented an appeal to the Sami Parliament to recognize its responsibility in the situation I described. More precisely, I sought a holistic media policy in our highest elected body. It is not entirely correct to say that our organization and institutions haven't been concerned with the media situation, but it has appeared until now that the attitude has been that this is an area that someone else must take responsibility for. As far as radio and TV go, the Sami have limited the engagement until now to sending regular inquiries to NRK, and refrained from being concrete in demands made to the state institution. The Sami have, in other words, demanded, and with justification, a better and expanded media offering, but what the offering should more concretely include has not yet been disclosed. The results of the demands, one could say, are the radio and TV media we have today.

In regards to other media our organizations, and later the Sami Parliament, have also followed up on Sami initiatives and contributed to our having at least a couple newspapers and a publishing house which are developing into a Sami national publisher. In this picture belongs also the work to establish a permanent Sami journalist education at the Sami College in Guovdageaidnu/Kautokeino, a program that is under development today.

NSR's Sami Parliament delegation adopted, in addition, the idea of working out a complete Sami media policy and promised to work out a Sami media announcement which will be put before the Sami Parliament's plenary. We'll see.

References:

Finnmark Dagblad, Hammerfest, 14.5. 1994.

Heatta, Nils Johan. (prošeaktajođiheaddji) 1992. *Rapporta Sámi Radio jagi 2000 vuostá,* Kárášjohka.

Heatta, Nils Johan, Nousuniemi, Juhani, Sikku, Nils Henrik. 1995. Samekanalen. *En utredning om etablering av en samnordisk samisk radiokanal,* Enare/-

197

Karasjok/Kiruna.

Min Áigi, Kárášjohka, 11.5. 1994.

NRK Radio long-term plan, approved by NRK's board, Aug. 25.

Sámediggi 1994. *Sámediggeplána* 1994-1997.

"Samer og informasjon," Program for Samisk medieseminar i Alta 12.3-14.3. 1980. NSR's archive, marked "Sáme Media"

Thomas, Ned. 1973 / 1991. The Welsh Extremist. *Modern Welsh Politics, Literature and Society,* Y Lolfa, Talybont.

Harald Gaski

Voice in the Margin[1]:

A Suitable Place for a Minority Literature?[2]

In America these days one can find a Sami-American journal, named *Báiki*. The Sami term means either "place" or "home," and is more or less a synonym for the term *ruoktu*. I would like to start by circling a bit around the different levels of meaning of the word "place" in Sami in an attempt to give you a sense of the associations the word in itself brings about for a Sami reader or listener. These associations may also express an understanding of the role of place among the Sami, meaning here a problematizing of the concept of "place" in a Sami world-view. A place needs borders to surround it to make it distinct compared to other places, or at least the notion of a place usually has some kind of a linkage to a geographical area or territory. How does this fit into the Sami use of the terms *báiki* and *ruoktu?* And how does this in turn relate to the Sami-American journal I mentioned in the beginning of this article?

I'll approach an answer to these questions indirectly, using Sami ways of getting close to a reply by responding through devious routes. That means I have to test your patience and invite you on a trip consisting of digressions. All of you probably know that the Sami way of telling a story is to tell *a lot of* stories simultaneously – one digression leading into another one into another one and so on. But you can rest assured that a Sami story always returns to its original point. So finally we'll return to the Sami-American magazine. On the other hand, I can't promise you anything about the time it'll take to finish my story, because – as you may know – the Sami conception of time may differ a bit from the linearity of seconds, minutes and hours in the Western world.

According to the most thorough Sami dictionary[3] *báiki* means "place, haunt, whereabouts, inhabited place," but also in one Sami dialect "farm" or "home" and in yet another dialect it may be understood as a "family tent with all its accessories." Furthermore *báiki* may mean "part, piece or section." *Ruoktu* in the same dictionary is explained as "whereabouts, place of residence, habitation, home."[4] The dictionary also includes some examples meant to clarify the use of the term, for instance using the case system of Sami language in connection with *ruoktu* to denote the opposite of work with the reindeer herd far afield. When you are *ruovttus* – at home – you are not far away out on the high plains of the tundra, meaning at least that you are not away from your tent, which in this context implies "home" – even though you still may be far away from your permanent residence, if you at all have a permanent base which could be signified as your home. Thus the binary pair home/away is established; home being the place where you find shelter from bad weather, the place where you eat and sleep in contrast away which is out herding the reindeer on their grazing land, which may be a bit away from the tent, the *lávvu* or *goahti*. (To make it even more complicated, I could in a certain way claim that I am at home wherever I lecture, because I am doing the same then as I do at home at the University of Tromsø – coping to make border-crossings between cultures comprehensible, or maybe rather to stay on the borderline, because that is where all the fun takes place. Therefore a more or less traditional Sami upbringing in a contemporary Norwegian society in a way gives a person more than two legs to stand on, because what one gets is a rather confident rooting and foundation in both of the cultures; one stands with both legs in both cultures).

These examples represent, of course, an over-simplified illustration of the problematics associated with the whole thinking around place, home and residence in connection with a – at least previously – nomadic culture. This down-to-earth philosophy also signifies the background against which we have to view Nils-Aslak Valkeapää's sequence of poetry, "My Home is in my Heart" from the lyrical work *Trekways of the Wind*. In this poem Nils-Aslak is *not* performing a Country & Western song, even though the title may take your thoughts in that direction. He is, on the contrary, trying to explain a different way of viewing the whole concept of utilizing nature in such a way that nature provides you with the necessities of good living, while remaining undamaged.

In this fairly long poem Valkeapää expresses the views of a nature-based culture when it comes to the question of ownership of land and water, the clashing of totally different notions of closeness to the places a person moves in, and most of all the feeling of inadequacy and impossibility in reaching across with an explanation as to why the whole surrounding – including landscapes, people, weather, the bushes, the lakes – why it all is a part of a person, an inseparable part of that person's whole identity: "My home is in my heart / it migrates with me / ...You know it brother / you understand sister / but what do I say to strangers / who spread out everywhere / how shall I answer their questions / that come from a different world." The concept of "place," the notion of "home" is dealt with in this poem – into the core of the matter, a Sami or a Native American probably would say, whereas a "Westerner" would call it romanticizing – a naivistic or may be a nativist view – which is totally out-of-date and marginalized in today's modern society.

This is exactly the matter that soon ought to become a theme for discussion in the approach to indigenous literatures, especially in the academic deliberations on Sami, Native American, Aboriginal and other indigenous peoples' writings: Does their voice represent an important link to the most fundamental issues of today's world; namely a consideration of the current state of the Earth and how that effects our possibilities to secure a decent life for our descendants? Or is Western man so proud, arrogant and insensitive to the voices representing primordial cares and values of our existence as human beings, and thus relatives to all other living species, that he doesn't want to listen – he just refuses to consider it at all? The way he does

201

this is by defining the themes and values of indigenous literature as backward, romantic, naivistic, marginal and out-of-date concerning form, style and tecniques. The way he manages to do this is by using the power of definition: deciding what is in at the moment, what is the most interesting, challenging way of writing, what is the most up-to-date form to use to be most recent and innovative, and by doing so, the "Westerner" is fully able to prove that the natural man doesn't write this way, and therefore his literature is not sufficiently interesting – be the content of the indigenous message as important as it may, you have to find a way to express yourself that makes you "digestable" for the rest of us, meaning "the West" of us...

This reminds me of something you might call just another digression, but still, please allow me this last one, and I promise to return to the main course. You know we Sami people are in an odd position in the world – an indigenous people traditionally, culturally and politically, but still we are "white" in regard to color. All the rest of the indigenous world differ visually from White Man, except the "White Indians of Scandinavia," i.e. the Sami people. Ironically many whites do their utmost to get a tan, really putting an effort into becoming darker. This was the point which a Canadian Indian singer by the name of Shingoose was amuzing himself with at the third general assembly of the World Council of Indigenous Peoples in Canberra in the spring of 1980. I was a young student and the editor of a Sami cultural magazine at that time covering the cultural part of the conference program. I remember very well this Canadian Indian singer who had such marvellous success at the evening performances with a song called "Thank God, I'm a Natural Man." I still remember part of the text, because I made a short portrait of the singer and the songwriter for my magazine, expressing the recurring Sami frustration about being so white in the indigenous world. The refrain of the song was; "I've got a natural tan / 'cause I'm a natural man. / You're welcome to be like me / but I don't want to be like you." For the Samis present, the phrase was both *in*clusive and *ex*clusive, because as long as we were wearing our *gaktis,* our

202

traditional Sami clothing, we were part of the indigenous group, everyone could see we looked different from the "white" people attending the conference, but the moment we took off our *gaktis,* we looked "white." There were in fact voices at the conference expressing scepticism towards the Sami, because of our "whiteness." We lack the natural tan, but we still claim to be part of the culture of the natural man.

So, where does all this talk eventually bring me? It brings me *home,* because in my heart too, is my *ruoktu,* my *báiki,* and it migrates with me. Nils-Aslak Valkeapää's poem and a play with words was the reason why *Báiki* was picked out to be the the the name of the Sami-American journal. In the promoting of the magazine, the editors have translated the term to mean "the Home That Lives in the Heart," meaning that you always bring your background, your surroundings, your family and friends along wherever you travel – meaning also that you have a home everywhere you go.

Let me then proceed to being more specific about Sami literature, but also situate it in the literary universe of the indigenous peoples. I'll start by referring to a few of the most profound Native American authors, continuing with an Aboriginal writer from Australia, taking a closer look at the theorizations concerning the research conducted on indigenous texts by one of the most outstanding non-indigenous theorists in this field, and then finally ending up with a Sami poet, who is innovative, experimental and at the same time a real traditionalist.

I am doing it this way very deliberately to underline the built-in paradoxes in the situation for Sami literature in Scandinavia and for that matter for indigenous people's literature in North America as well as in Australia and New Zealand. On the one hand we are dealing with a *regional* literature, which in many cases is also marginalized in the public sphere, especially considered from the so-called center, it being either the established literary institutions or just the general view of the regional rural rustic countryside outside Oslo, New York, Los Angeles and Canberra. On the other hand the

203

literature in the regions naturally is not at all marginal for the inhabitants of the de-central areas as far as literature in any sense is paid attention to anymore. Regional literature is the voice of the margin, and probably because of its topical orientations it is categorized as belonging to one area, dealing with more or less predictable subjects; in other words it is committed to its region (its "o-region," meaning; *origin*). As far as this characterization is connected with the thematic content of regional literature, the definition may be correct, but in this sense urban literature is also regional, because it as well is thematically limited to its own geographical setting and topics, being the *non*-rural life of people. Evidently nowadays city-life is relevant for more people than stories connected with fisheries and reindeer herding; but still, literature is not just about the exterior, not just the plot, so a book about for instance the hardships of surviving as an anti-hero in Samiland may interest a reader just as much as a story about an urban cowboy. In spite of this rather rhetorical point about all literatures being regional in the end, I am – of course – fully aware of the existing power structures ultimately defining what is "most-modern" on the literary stage. These powers are seldom situated in the region, neither are they especially occupied with the *geographical* margins, so to the extent regional literature at all manages to place itself within the reach of the latest trends, it is in most cases despite of its marginal burden rather than because of any additional points for its de-central origin or incipience.

This of course is a banality. What is more important, however, is the possibility of transcending the limits put there by definitions, meaning in this context expressing what is regional and what is not. In the case of Sami literature, it exists and is produced in four different countries, thus rejecting the whole idea of a literature confined only to a small locality. On the other hand it *is* of course local, and it *is* connected to Sami language, culture and societal life – which in turn *is* marginalized in the Scandinavian and Russian cultural and political systems. In that sense, Sami literature *is* "A

Voice in the Margin" as well as "A Voice *of* the Margin."

What makes Sami literature interesting in an *international* context, is its affinity to indigenous peoples' literatures in the rest of the world. Since the 1970s, there has existed a collaboration between different aboriginal populations through organizations like the World Council of Indigenous Peoples. The activity has not just involved politics. Cultural festivals, putting up joint art exhibits and theater performances, common research projects and student exchange programs are some of the benefits from the shared efforts. Recently we have even gotten the first translations of contemporary Sami literature into English, meaning that Sami literature finally joins the international arena with its own voice *from* the margin.[5] Until now the Sami have been able to enjoy the writings of their native brothers and sisters elsewhere, without having the opportunity to share their own literature with the rest of the world. Now, at a time when things are changing in this field, we start to see the commonalities and similarities between the different indigenous literatures, in thematics, in the literary situation and to some extent even in regard to content. The identity question in all its nuances is naturally a common theme, as is the recurring problematics of the minority situation. The language issue is another returning theme – to know it or not to know it. There is, however, still another dimension to it in the matter of how to read it – even though you don't know it – inbetween the lines, in a more or less "hidden communication" with your primary readers, the ones familiar with the cultural codes of the author, meaning one of your own people, who understands more than what is expressed *in* the lines due to cultural affinity (Gaski 1988: 18-20).

Self-identification is often regarded as insufficient to determine who really is an indigenous person. To illustrate this problem as seen from the point of view of the Native American, I want to quote from Louis Owens' book *Other Destinies. Understanding the American Indian Novel,* where he cites Karen I. Blu:

For Whites, blood is a substence that can be either racially pure or racially polluted. Black blood pollutes White blood absolutely, so that in the logical extreme, one drop of Black blood makes an otherwise White man Black.... White ideas about "Indian blood" are less formalized and clearcut.... It may take only one drop of Black blood to make a person a Negro, but it takes a lot of Indian blood to make a person a "real" Indian. *(The Lumbee Problem: The Making of an American Indian.* Cambridge University Press 1980:25. Here quoted from Owens 1992: 3-4).

The Choctaw-Cherokee novelist and professor of Native American literature, Louis Owens, continues;

Identity for Native Americans is made more complex yet by the fact that the American Indian in the world consciousness is a treasured invention, a gothic artifact evoked like the "powwows" in Hawthorne's "Young Goodman Brown" out of the dark reaches of the continent to replace the actual native, who, painfully problematic in real life, is supposed to have long since vanished. (1992: 4).

Owens goes on to explain that it is at the disjuncture between myth and reality that American Indian novelists most often take aim, and cites the Chippewa writer and professor of Native American literature, Gerald Vizenor, when he says, "I'm still educating an audience."

Owens' theme is the American Indian, but the case of the Indians is very similar with the situation of a lot of indigenous peoples in the world, so his point is applicable as a description of the minority-versus-majority relationship between the Fourth World and Western societies as a whole:

The problem of identity comprehends centuries of colonial and post-colonial displacement, often brutally enforced peripherality, cultural denigration – including especially a harsh privileging of English over tribal languages – and systematic oppression by the monocentric "westering" impulse in America. (4).

Against this background Native American literature represents a process of reconstruction, of self-discovery and cultural recovery. Thus the identity question becomes "the central issue and theme for the contemporary [American] Indian novelist – in every case a mixed-blood who must come to terms in one form or another with peripherality as well as both European and Indian ethnicity," Owens asserts and refers to James Clifford's suggestion about ethnic identity as always being "mixed, relational, and inventive." "We are what we imagine," as the Kiowa writer and Pulitzer prize recipient N. Scott Momaday has put it.

Another alienating factor for a lot of the indigenous writing is the language issue, what language to write in – the mother tongue or one of the majority languages? What about all the writers who have lost the minority language, or at least lack the degree of proficiency necessary to produce fiction in it? The Aboriginal writer and scholar Mudrooroo Narogin, formerly Colin Johnson, was the first "black-fella" to publish a book in Australia. He says, "It is a curious fate to write for a people not one's own and stranger still to write for the conquerors of one's people"(1990:148). Mudrooroo explores the Aboriginal writer's dilemma with language itself when the "mother tongue" has been lost, when standard English has been, by social and educational custom, unattainable to all but a privileged few of the Aboriginal population, and when the Creole patterns of Aboriginal speech are subject to erasure by white editors. Mudrooroo opens his book, *Writing from the Fringe,* with an assertion that pinpoints the political burden carried by any Aboriginal writer today: "Aboriginal Literature begins as a cry from the heart directed at the whiteman. It is a cry for justice and for a better deal, a cry for understanding and an asking to be understood"(1).

Writing in the language of the dominant culture leads to a re-orientation. This is a point also made by Louis Owens: "For the Indian author," he says, "writing within consciousness of the con-textual background of a nonliterate culture, every word written in English represents a collaboration of sorts as well as a reorientation (conscious or unconscious) from the paradigmatic world of oral tradition to the syntagmatic reality of written language." (6).

In the example from the United States it is the privileged class that produces fiction. In Owens' words, "Contemporary American Indian writers have indeed most often permanently entered that class, possessing as they do a consistently high level of education (almost always at least one college degree) and mastery of English, a fact that certainly adds complexity to the overarching question of cultural identity." (7).

The Sami and Inuit case is, on the contrary, that very few of the indigenous writers have any higher education at all. Still the identity question is a major theme in all their literary production, but the fiction texts themselves may not to the same degree be used as a battlefield between different approaches towards the question of identity as the case may be in Native American literature.

Among Sami authors the complicated language issue has been articulated in a self-contradictory phrase: The biggest problem for the Sami writers is the fact that they cannot write – meaning that they haven't got any education to write in their own language. I will not go any further into the possible consequences of this particular statement, but its background is easily understandable in light of historical facts. Most Sami writers produce their texts *in* Sami, a language that has been taught in selected schools only since the early 1970s. This means that just a few of the currently established Sami writers have ever had any schooling in Sami. Consequently most have not mastered Sami orthography, nor have they learned anything in school about their own background and culture to make them feel proud enough to write about it. What they know about Sami issues stems mostly from what they have learned at home as children and what they have experienced themselves growing up and living in a Sami area. A lot of the education they had in the majority language they did not catch or care about because it was alien, it did not have any reference to their own lives and it did not prepare them for a life and a livelihood in the cold, harsh Sapmi. Thus a lot of Sami youngsters in the 1950s, 60s and even 70s did not get what they should have gotten out of school. They were asked to reject their own background, but the alternative they were given was not explained in an intelligible way, so it passed by as well. To try to find out what really happened, to discover and explain both to themselves and to their readers, or maybe more correctly, to investigate together with their readers what Sami culture really means and represents for today's people, is a major project for Sami artists. It is also a recovery project, a search for identity, the native identity that would have given them assurance and self-confidence. (Gaski 1993: 122-3 and 126-7).

In an age when traditions change, when the continuity between old and new is scarcely taken care of and the wisdom of the old ways is forgotten, new media, such as books, serve the indispensable function of preservation and celebration among indigenous peoples. The oral tradition has to be written down to be remembered, otherwise the whole orally transmitted history will vanish with the dispersion and expansion of modern mass media.

Changing social and economic realities have brought about new challenges for the role of art in traditional societies. Arts are asserting their position as identity-markers and as a way of communicating internal matters within minority cultures. The renewal of Sami culture, a development project that takes into account the basis and benefits of traditional knowledge and behavior, may also be part of a globalization of Sami values and thoughts. Instead of shutting the door to the outside world, the current trend may very well be a means of reaching out to the world with the message of the first peoples. As put by Harald Eidheim, a Norwegian anthropologist with a thorough knowledge of various aspects of the Sami cultural situation:

> One aspect of this (globalization) involves the judgement and eventual "authorization" of new and contemporary manifestations of Saminess – manifestations which some call "cultural cloning." That is to say,

inventions in which traditional Sami idioms of various classes in a way are combined or coordinated with other, alien idioms to make constructs with "double signature" so to speak. Several such constructs have been discovered from the outside and circulate inter-culturally as signs of contemporary Sami imagination, life style, cultural creativity and national self-assertion. The most conspicuous have to do with music, painting, sculpture and literature. (..) A prominent example is the internationally famed film *Ofelaš (Pathfinder)* directed by Nils Gaup. (Eidheim 1992:27).

Being a Sami scholar in the field of comparative literature represents an interesting approach to research on Sami texts, especially on traditional material like the yoik lyrics. Yoik is a kind of chanting, the traditional vocal genre of the Sami.[6] Knowing the cultural background of the yoik, and, at the same time, knowing the literary methods normally used for the interpretation of textual materials, may serve as a two-fold approach to Sami texts, where cultural background, linguistic skills in Sami and literary methods converge and enrich each other to understand more of the texts than knowing only one of the skills would allow. There is, nevertheless, a residue left in the text – something, which is not easily explicated through the methodical exposition of the subject. This something I like to think of as being a more or less culturally internal code or mode, which is hard to catch without a broad knowledge of the background and context of the story, song or myth.

Being aware of this extra potential of the text, and also being able to explicate it, is of course the advantage of the "insider." This is furthermore the part of all artistic performance – and understanding – that represents the specific values of each culture, and thus is celebrated as a certain kind of cultural wealth. Still, be these internal matters as important as they may, the real interesting point of this "internality" only comes into its own when it is made communicable for a larger audience. In regard to literary interpretations of texts celebrating limited openness, some may only want to emphasize their esoteric potential, while others prefer to try to make them more communicative.

An important dimension regarding for example the Sami yoik is its exclusive and, to some extent, excluding ability as a communicative form. These double layers of communication have both the goal and intention that a Sami should be able to understand more than a non-Sami. This is in part what Sami artists attempt to accomplish in their work: one desires to say more to the Sami than to the others.This need not imply a condescending attitude toward the others, but should be considered an outgrowth of taking Sami cultural history seriously – that one, for example, continues in the esthetic process that the Sami have always enjoyed playing with. When applied to language usage of all kinds, this suggests finding a means of communicating within the group, so that the Sami take more pleasure in that which is spoken and written than do those who do not fully understand the code. The idea behind such a form of communication is that those inside the culture comprehend all from the beginning, while those who do not understand may actually come to understand to the extent that they are no longer uninformed, but hardly ever become 'completely' informed.

This is a problematic stance to take, I admit, and I am not at all sure that I myself believe in a cultural positioning implying a dichotomous division between the "partly-informed" and the "fully-informed," especially not when it comes to interpreting, as it ultimately will concerning artistic expressions. There is probably also a need to differentiate between criticism per se and the intended perception of a more or less culturally implicit message one may find in traditional communicative forms like the yoik. Even though the yoik text's primary aim and content, for instance, may be just to amuse a locally limited audience, the text in itself may still contain other more subtle levels which may be interpreted otherwise by "outsiders," be the outsider another Sami from a different community or a "real" outsider in the shape of a foreign critic, whose only involvement is with the text. In this case it is at least conceivable that the not-fully-informed might yet offer insights that the (presumably) fully-informed might not, meaning that even though the

211

insider is likely to have a cultural advantage in understanding the text's full potential, he or she may still be blind to details and layers that may prove to be important for the interpretation of the text as a literary product. It may sound strange, I agree, to differ between a "primary-adressee's" *understanding* of a traditional expression like the Sami yoik on the one hand, and a, let us say, scholarly *interpretation* of the same text, where all parts of the text are thoroughly scrutinized. Still, I think, that the differentiation is not just possible, it is also desirable, because it takes into account not only the intended contents of a message, but also makes room for a reading of the possible un-intentional implications and connotations of the text.

I am not trying to underestimate or minimalize the importance of the inside-reading of a text – I'll immediately return to proving the opposite – I'm just problematizing the difficult *positioning of criticism* in this picture, not totally willing to accept the exclusiveness of a so-called indigenous criticism on the one hand, and on the other pointing out the shortcomings of a merely outside, and "neutral" criticism, claiming nothing else but the text in front of you to be relevant for the "correct" and full interpretation.

In my view this kind of debate is a conscious and productive way for the indigenous societies to communicate with "Western" theorizing while still insisting on the importance of "native understandings," but still be willing to engage in theoretical discussions with open-mindedness and an *in*-clusive attitude towards outsiders, who see our points, but still want both us and themselves to clarify the groundings we all stand on in an attempt to get to an even better level of understanding. In the Sami case, there is a need to take into account a culturally – and linguistically – based criticism of Sami literature in addition to, or rather as a part of, more established methodical readings. Otherwise one runs the danger of leaving the Sami silent even in the literary discourse pertaining to Sami issues and thematics.

At this point in history, however, we have an interesting counterpart to the *native* experiences represented by non-native scholars who want to understand indigenous culture and literature, and who from their theoretical point of view talk about Otherness as a challenge to *their* scientific approach and ability to understand and explain the native text. This is an interesting contrast, and as far as I am able to judge, a productive approach in the contemporary relationship between "us" and "them," between the native and the non-native world-views. One of the most prominent representatives of these new ethnocritics is the American scholar Arnold Krupat, who has aptly entitled one of his books in this field *Ethnocriticism*. In this book Krupat makes a serious attempt at clearing the ground for a theoretical and analytical approach to studying Native American texts on a fuller and more proper scale than the dichotomous way it mostly has been practised till now. His aim is "to urge the decon- struction of all dichotomized paradigms of us/them, West/Rest type, and so to undo Manichean allegories at every level." (Krupat 1992: 238-39).

> ... ethnocriticism does not offer itself as a master narrative," Krupat ex- plains, but "Given its frontier condition of liminality or betweenness, ethnocriticism by its very nature must test any appeals to "reason," "science," "knowledge," or "truth" it would make in relation to Other or non-Western constructions of these categories, or, for that matter, to any alternative categories Others may propose (27).

Krupat stresses that his ethnocriticism is not an "indigenous" criticism ("unwilling to speak *for* the Indian and unable to speak *as* an Indian"), but on the other hand he also asserts that there does not really exist any pure and mere indigenous criticism of Native Ameri- can literature, and he even questions whether it *can* or ever *should* be worked out (1992: 44-45). Compared to the above mentioned contrast in the shift of interest in native literature, it is pleasing, seen from the indigenous viewpoint, to observe the limitations Western researchers themselves see for their new theories, acknowledging the power relations between a minority and a majority, and also acknowledging their own position in this power relation. Krupat for instance says, "For all that ethnocriticism wishes to engage on an equal footing with Native literary practice, it cannot help but do so in a context of vastly unequal power relations" (186). The institutional power is still in the hands of Western researchers, but the power of truth in the indigenous peoples' practices is about to be recognized. In Krupat's words,

> Native modes of knowing and understanding are not well known, and that is in large measure because they have not been formulated as analytic or critical modes *apart* from the verbal performances they would know and understand. (44).

"I mean to say," he continues a hundred and forty pages later,

> that contemporary singing and storytelling goes on in communities that use those performances as means of affirming and validating their identities as communities – communities, which, insofar as they are traditionally oriented, do not separate those stories from their performers, audiences, and occasions, and so have no reason to develop any distinctive category of "criticism" about them. This is not in the least to say that Indian people have no ideas or thoughts about "literature" they perform or participate in; it is to say that they have no need to produce a body of knowledge *about* it that is separate and *apart* from it. (187).

Sami literature and Inuit literature from Greenland are mostly written in their respective mother tongues, and only through translations do they reach other readers. Translation is of course a theme in its own right, but this is not the place to go into the problems of translation. Yet I feel an urge to state the difference between contemporary Sami and Inuit literature on the one hand and Native American, Maori and Aboriginal literature on the other when it comes to the language question. It is a different challenge to write books in the minority language for an audience consisting partly of illiterates, partly of neglectors and numbering at most a few thousand readers, as compared to writing books in English with a potential readership of millions. It is easy to understand that one moves in much more intimate and probably more sympathetic circles writing in one's mother tongue and almost being able to know every reader, than does the person who brings out a book in English even though it may be through one of the small and alternative presses. The primary addressee for both categories of writers may well be the minority readers, but the Sami and Inuit writers know for sure that before their books are translated into other languages, they will only get across with their message to those knowledgeable in the minority languages.

Does this difference in any way influence the writing, the use of language or the scope and theme of the book? To discuss this matter I will use as my example a poem from the award-winning book, *Beaivi, Áhčážan (Solen, min far; The Sun, My Father),* by the Sami multimedia artist, Nils-Aslak Valkeapää.

Nils-Aslak Valkeapää created a new interest in the Sami yoik by innovatively combining it with popular music, jazz and even classical music in an attempt to bring it closer to the taste of "modern" man. He did this to revitalize Sami traditions, to make sure they would continue as vital and intriguing elements of present-day culture. The yoik does not belong in a museum, it ought to live on as an important medium and a symbol for the Sami. To many indigenous peoples traditional singing is a part of literature, and even an important basis for modern poetry, just like story-telling creates the foundation for a lot of prose fiction. This is the case for the Sami, too. The yoik texts build on a tradition of their own, not a scholarly expressed and explained literary system of different "-isms," but a thousand year-old sense of belonging to a place, a family, and a people. The yoik is a way of remembering – it connects a person with the innermost feelings expressed in the theme of the yoik, and may thus communicate between times, persons, and landscapes.

In Valkeapää's view, the time has come to renew this tradition through innovation in traditional artistic forms and genres. One example of his many-levelled linguistic play is poem No. 272 in *The*

Sun, My Father. The poem spans seven and a half pages, where the words spread out more and more on the pages till they finally are scattered all over pages 5 and 6. On pages 6, 7 and 8 are found some dotted lines that, at the end, form one dotted line. The poem is a typographical play as well as a linguistic challenge to every Sami with a high proficiency in the specific terminology regarding reindeer names, because the poem in fact represents a reindeer herd on the move. The herdsman is leading the flock in the opposite direction of our reading of the book, that is, we meet the herd on our wandering on the tundras (read: the pages of the book). We pass the herd, which has spread all over pages 5 and 6, because the reindeer are resting and grazing on those pages. When we further continue on our trip, we meet with the tracks and the footprints of the passing reindeer. The text in italics consists of onomatopoetics from the moving herd, as well as of descriptive poetic echoing sounds of the natural surroundings. The plain text represents different reindeer, according to their age, their appearance, whether they are male or female, whether they are spotted or have any other kind of special marks and so on. The Sami language has an enormous vocabulary for describing reindeer, just as it has approximately 150 different terms to precisely identify different kinds of snow. Also in terms of topography, kinship relations and metaphorical circumlocutions for predators like the bear and the wolf in connection to taboos and beliefs, the Sami language has a wealth of terms and names. This fact is of course a richness and a challenge for poetic use of the language, like that which Valkeapää has displayed in this particular poem.

As a matter of fact, a poem like No. 272 is impossible to translate into any other language. At least, I do not know about any other language with exactly the same kind of terminology for reindeer names. In any case the poem was left untranslated in the Scandinavian and English renditions of Valkeapää's book, because those languages lack the equivalent terms for reindeer. Thus the limitations of the majority languages are laid bare, they are unable to match or rival Sami in regard to explaining with exact preciseness the content and consequences of Sami experiences. Accordingly the Sami readers are reassured about the fitness and importance of their own language as the best and most useful tool to cover the needs of Sami communication. The larger claim to make would be to assume that the sort of sophistication shown regarding reindeer is potentially applicable to other phenomena as well,[7] so one does not have to be particularly interested in reindeer to be impressed with the intellectual complexity of a language that can do what Sami can do in one word. This fact may contribute to boosting an exploration into the Sami language in an attempt to use these succinct terms in other fields as well as to examine the accuracy and exactness of scientific terms and language in general, not least in regard to arctic experiences.

For non-Sami readers the untranslated poem may at first sight represent an amusing and exotic example of the peculiarity of a totally different language, but it might as well provoke because the poem remains unintelligible to someone who doesn't read or speak Sami, with the exception of the typography. There is, admittedly, a difference between having the poem in a Sami poetry book and reading it there, and finding the same poem untranslated in a Scandinavian or English version of the book. What originally would be interpreted as a humoristic, but still realistic and fully possible thing to do in the Sami book, suddenly appears as an ironic commentary upon the inability of the majority languages to fully express Sami experience. The poem becomes politicized, esthetics turn into ideology. The example may well serve as a basis for further theorizing, not only about two different language codes, but more fundamentally as evidence for two different ways of viewing the world. If that is so, and in fact there are a lot of fields where Sami and Scandinavian languages are distant from each other when it comes to describing the essence of the experience, the condition in itself is actually so interesting that it should absolutely inspire one to more thorough analysis into the matter. Theoretical approaches are at least always dependent on an abstract language, and if it is true that the linguistic explanation of the things we see is quite different between two separate cultures, then consequently this fact must have an influence on the theories we choose and the methods we create to view and interpret our surroundings.

Therefore a poem of reindeer may enable the Sami reader to ironize with the assimilationist: "Hi there, wait a minute! Didn't you tell us that our language is an inferior one? So what do you call a four-year-old male reindeer with a white spot on its leg, and with the antlers pointing forward? In one word, please!"

1   I have borrowed the first part of the title from the name of a book by Arnold Krupat, *The Voice in the Margin: Native American Literature and the canon*, 1989. Like American Indian literature Sami literature is also regarded as marginal writing, and must therefore cope on unequal terms with the expectations of the "established readers" and their views of what kind of literature may be regarded as canonical. I return later to consider the use of different prepositions in connection with the title of this paper, all of them still expressing the same marginality concerning the literature dealt with here.

2   Originally given as a talk at a conference on "Literary Regionalism: The Case of Norway" at the Chicago Humanities Institute at the University of Chicago, February 9-10, 1996. A somewhat different version of this article has been printed in the conference report, *Places Within, Places Beyond. Norwegian Regionalism in Literature*, 1996

3   Konrad Nielsen *Lapp Dictionary*, Vol. I: 106, Oslo 1932-62 (1979), Universitetsforlaget.

4
    Op.cit. Vol. III: 334.

5   Let me in this context in addition to Valkeapää's book of poetry, mention an anthology of contemporary Sami prose and poetry, titled *In the Shadow of the Midnight Sun. Contemporary Sami Prose and Poetry*, 1996.

6   See more about Sami yoik in my forthcoming article "The secretive text: Yoik lyrics as literature and tradition" in *Sami Folkloristics*, 1997.

7   Cf. Nils Jernsletten's article in this book on Sami traditional terminology
     concerning, among other things, snow, ice, and salmon.

References:

Báiki. An American Journal of Sami Living. 1991 Issue 1: 1-2. San Fransisco.

Eidheim, Harald. 1992. *Stages in the Development of Sami Selfhood,* Working
     Paper no. 7, Department of Social Anthropology, University of Oslo.

Gaski, Harald. 1988. "The Free Sounds of the Joik in Writing." *News from the Top
     of the World. Norwegian Literature Today,* No. 1: 17-25. Oslo.

Gaski, Harald. 1993. "The Sami People: The 'White Indians' of Scandinavia."
     American Indian Culture and Research Journal, Vol. 17, No. 1: 115-128. Los
     Angeles, UCLA.

Gaski, Harald. 1996. "Voice in the Margin. A suitable Place for a Minority
     Literature," *Places Within, Places Beyond. Norwegian Regionalism in
     Literature,* W. Griswold and F. Engelstad (eds.), Institute for Social Research,
     Oslo: 92-108.

Gaski, Harald. 1997. "The secretive text: Yoik lyrics as literature and tradition."
     Sami Folkloristics: Research history and interpretations, (forthcoming Spring
     97), Åbo, Nordic Institute of Folkore.

Jernsletten, Nils. 1997. "Sami Traditional Terminology: Professional Terms
     Concerning Salmon, Reindeer and Snow." *Sami Culture in a New Era: The
     Norwegian Sami Experience,* H. Gaski (ed.), Karasjok, Davvi Girji OS.

Krupat, Arnold. 1992. *Ethnocriticism. Ethnography, History, Literature,*
     Berkeley, University of California Press.

Krupat, Arnold. 1989. *The Voice in the Margin: Native American Literature and
     the Canon,* Berkeley, University of California Press.

Narogin, Mudrooroo. 1990. *Writing from the Fringe. A Study of Modern
     Aboriginal Literature,* Melbourne, Hyland House.

Nielsen, Konrad. 1979. *Samisk (lappisk) ordbok / Lapp Dictionary,* Vol. I-V 1932-
     62, Oslo (reprinted in 1979 by Universitetsforlaget).

Owens, Louise. 1992. *Other Destinies. Understanding the American Indian
     Novel,* Norman, University of Oklahoma Press.

Valkeapää, Nils-Aslak. 1985. *Ruoktu váimmus,* Kautokeino, DAT.

Valkeapää, Nils-Aslak. 1994. *Trekways of the Wind* (transl. by R.Salisbury, L.Nordström and H.Gaski), Kautokeino, DAT. (Distribution in the USA by the University of Arizona Press, Tucson).

Valkeapää, Nils-Aslak. 1989. *Beaivi, Áhčážan,* Kautokeino, DAT.

Valkeapää, Nils-Aslak. 1990. *Solen, min far,* Kautokeino, DAT.

Valkeapää, Nils-Aslak. 1997. *The Sun, My Father.* Kautokeino, DAT, (Distribution in the USA by University of Washington Press, Seattle).

Notes on contributors

Harald Eidheim (b. 1925), social anthropologist, former Professor of Sami Studies at the University of Tromsø and Associate Professor of social anthropology at the University of Oslo. He has done fieldwork in several Sami areas since the 1950s and published on cultural and ethno-political aspects of modern Sami life. Most well-known is his *Aspects of the Lappish Minority Situation*, 1971. In the capacity of Professor Emeritus he is currently active as teacher and supervisor for graduate and Ph.D. students at the University of Tromsø.

Einar Niemi (b. 1943), Professor of History at the University of Tromsø. He started his career as high school teacher. Has had positions as university lecturer and county curator (museums and cultural heritage). Has published widely nationally and interationally within the history of ethnic minorities, migration, social and cultural history and regional history, with main focus on Northern Scandinavia. Among his books are *Den finske fare*, 1981 (on the Norwegian minority policy in the north, in collaboration with K.E. Eriksen), *Vadsøs historie*, 1983 (regional study), and *Pomor*, 1992 (on Russian-Norwegian relations).

Nils Jernsletten (b. 1934), Professor of Sami Language at the University of Tromsø. Jernsletten grew up in a small Sami village on the banks of the Tana River, where salmon fishing has long been an important source of income. First educated as a teacher, he has, for most of his professional life, been associated with Sami education. He is currently the head of the Sami Language Council, and was a member of the Sami Rights' Commission from 1981 till 1997.

Johan Klemet Hætta Kalstad (b. 1946), was a reindeer herder in his youth. After a period at the Ministry of Agriculture and Employment in Oslo, he moved back to his home community in Kautokeino to serve at the local government level. He is currently a Ph.D. candidate at the University of Tromsø researching the modernization of reindeer pastoralism in Northern Norway. His focus is on the management of commonland with emphasis on regulative and cognitive aspects of institutions maintaining sustainable development.

Vigdis Stordahl (b. 1951), Associate Professor at the Department of Child and Adolescent Psychiatry, School of Medicine at the University of Tromsø. Her main scope of research is Sami modernity; how the complex process of modernity is unfolding itself in cognitive as well as political level in today's Sami society – a matter which also is discussed in her doctoral dissertation, published in 1996, *Same i den moderne verden*. Another of her research topics is the field of transcultural psychiatry where her concern is how to develop more culturally sensitive psychiatric services for Sami children and youth.

Siv Kvernmo (b. 1955), trained in child and adolescent psychiatry and general practice in the Sami core areas. She is working on her Ph.D. dissertation at the Faculty of Medicine at the University of Tromsø. Her research interests include the influence of ethnic and cultural factors on emotional and mental health in indigenous adolescents, and psychiatric epidemiology.

Jan Henry Keskitalo (b. 1946), currently a Visiting Scholar at Western Washington University in Bellingham researching the relationship between primary education curricula and society and culture in selected Arctic communities. He has work experience from elementary teaching, teacher training and counseling in special education. He was President of The Sami Education Council 1987-1994, member of the Norwegian Cultural Council 1985-96 and the Board on Humanities and Social Sciences within the Norwegian Research Council 1993-96. He was Rector of the Sami College 1989-96.

John T. Solbakk (b. 1945), Research Fellow in Sami literature at the Sami Department, and Librarian Studies Department at the University of Tromsø. He is a former journalist and editor in Sami Radio and TV, as well as in a Sami newspaper 1973-81. He served as the head of a Sami press 1982-92, and is currently working on a Ph.D. project named "Literature as an Institution in Building up a Modern Culture for a Minority Nation" at the University of Tromsø.

Harald Gaski (b. 1955), Associate Professor of Sami Literature at the University of Tromsø, and the author and editor of several books and articles on Sami Literature and Culture. His research topics in addition to Sami literature, are oral tradition – especially the transition of yoik poetry into contemporary lyrics – and ethno-critical approaches to indigenous peoples' literature. Has also participated in translating Sami poetry into English. Latest book in English is the anthology *In the Shadow of the Midnight Sun. Contemporary Sami Prose and Poetry*, 1996.

Jo Ann Conrad (b. 1953). Although not contributing her own article, Conrad, as proof reader, and style and content advisor on the English versions of the articles significantly contributed to the final form of this volume. A Fulbright Scholar at the University of Tromsø the academic year 1996-97, Conrad is researching the topic of Sami identity management for her Ph.D. dissertation at the University of California, Berkeley.